Guiding Readers
Through Non-Fiction

Guiding Readers Through Non-Fiction

Effective Strategies for Small-Group Instruction

by Dave Leochko *and* Tom Rossi

PORTAGE & MAIN PRESS

Portage & Main Press acknowledges the financial support of the Government of Canada through the Book Publishing Industry Development Program (BPIDP) for our publishing activities.

Printed and bound in Canada by Friesens.

Illustrations and cover illustration: Jess Dixon

Book and cover design: Relish Design Studio Ltd.

LIBRARY AND ARCHIVES CANADA CATALOGUING IN PUBLICATION

Leochko, Dave, 1963-

   Guiding readers through non-fiction : effective strategies for small-group instruction/ Dave Leochko and Tom Rossi.

Includes bibliographical references and index.
ISBN 978-1-55379-124-9

1. Reading (Elementary) 2. Guided reading. I. Rossi, Tom
II. Title.

LB1050.377.L45 2007   372.41'62   C2007-902087-9

PORTAGE & MAIN PRESS

100 – 318 McDermot Ave.
Winnipeg, MB Canada R3A 0A2
Email: books@portageandmainpress.com
Tel: 204-987-3500
Toll-free: 1-800-667-9673
Fax-free: 1-866-734-8477

printed on 30% PCW paper

CONTENTS

INTRODUCTION

The times we live in influence our skills of reading. During the previous century, reading was a pleasurable pastime of the upper class of society or a part of the academic world, available to only a small segment of the population. In today's world, reading has maintained the aspect of pleasure, but access to reading has broadened to a wider audience. Reading continues to be a key feature in the academic world, but it is also an essential tool for everyone. It is now integral to our ability to function as a citizen of our society. The ability to make a livelihood or to manage a household often requires the ability to read. Indeed, the biggest change to reading in the past hundred years has been its functionality.

Reading is a part of daily life. It would be difficult to go through our regular routines without reading. With the move towards functionality of reading, there has been a shift in the popularity of genres of reading. Fiction has been replaced by non-fiction as our primary source of reading material. Forms of print that were scarce a hundred years ago saturate our world today. News magazines/ papers, cookbooks, manuals, journals, directions or instructions, and texts are commonplace today. The Internet is a continuous source for information to read on our screens. We are living in the information age and reading is an important part of obtaining that information.

Our schools are reflections of society and, as the focus of reading has shifted, so has the nature of reading methodologies in our schools evolved. Traditionally, non-fiction was assumed to be a part of content-based curricula such as science and social studies. It was also assumed that fiction was the main genre for developing reading skills. Non-fiction played a small part in the language arts program. Today, however, non-fiction material is an integral part of most curricula.

Teachers are aware that different skills are required for different forms of reading. The skills we use to read vary, depending on the purpose or intent of the reading. Those required for non-fiction are not necessarily the ones we use for fiction, and vice versa. The processes a student applies to a textbook are not the same as those used to engage in a novel. Non-fiction brings with it a different format and structure, which require other existing knowledge. As educators, it is our job to have students become as comfortable with, and knowledgeable about, non-fiction skills as they are with the processes they use for fiction. Our intention is to provide information and resources that will assist teachers in the job of teaching reading and providing students with the necessary skills for working with non-fiction material.

Reading non-fiction can be taught in a variety of ways, but one of the most effective teaching methodologies is small-group instruction. It allows teachers the opportunities to work more closely with students and assess their individual needs. Teachers are able to provide immediate feedback to the students and adapt material to fit the needs of each student. Of course, small-group instruction can have many different forms and there are many excellent practices for working with small groups. We have borrowed elements of the guided reading methodology to conduct our small-group instruction to help students learn about the nature of non-fiction and the key elements that go with non-fiction.

In this book, we hope to provide teachers with the information necessary for applying some of the practices of guided reading to their small-group instruction. We examine materials, structures, routines, goals and outcomes, assessment, and management. We created articles and essays as models of instruction that can be reproduced for classroom use. This book is intended as a resource to help teachers establish new practices or supplement existing ones with regards to small-group instruction. The materials are ready to use for grades four to seven students who are faced with increasing expectations to use non-fiction. The principles behind the practices discussed in the book can be adapted easily to fit the needs of students of other grades. We hope the material is as useful to other teachers as it has been to us.

CHAPTER ONE

THE NATURE OF NON-FICTION

Fiction is celebrated as a diverse form of writing, but non-fiction material is often considered to be one form. Non-fiction is treated as one of many different genres of literature, along with mystery, fantasy, adventure, and romance. In fiction, students are taught the elements of story, such as characterization, irony, and metaphor, among others. They are exposed to different features of a story, such as point of view, tense, and plot structure. In contrast, in many situations, non-fiction is narrowly defined as text that gives us information. Although this broad generalization is correct, there is much more to non-fiction.

Non-fiction is often described simply as an opposite to fiction. It is a much more complex system, rather than being merely a term in relation to an existing structure.

Non-fiction helps us understand the meaning of the world around and beyond us, through the sharing of factual content. Authors of non-fiction wish to share their experiences or expertise of the world with readers, using information they believe to be true. Non-fiction writing may be supported with elements such as graphs, pictures, or charts. Our world continually provides us with information, which suggests that non-fiction is a very diverse form of reading.

An analysis of non-fiction reveals four main components:

1. genre: purpose or intent of the material
2. structure: the format applied to the ideas
3. style: techniques and strategies applied to the writing
4. element: print features used to convey the message

From these four components, teachers create lessons and make decisions about the content with which students will work. These components are to be used as a starting point for planning. When non-fiction is divided into these four components, teachers are better able to select material on this basis and create a constructive purpose to each lesson.

When students understand the purpose of a non-fiction text, can identify the structure used, are aware of the style implemented, and make use of the features of the piece of writing, then they are using the necessary tools for being an effective reader of non-fiction.

There is a hierarchy for the components of non-fiction. Genre is the foundation. The application of the other components depends on the genre being used. It is one of the first lessons for students to learn—the purpose or intent of information must be identified, prior to applying the other components of non-fiction. The purpose will help the author and reader determine the structure, style, and elements.

NON-FICTION GENRES—PURPOSE AND INTENT

The first component of non-fiction is *genre*. The genres in non-fiction are as easily identifiable as those in fiction. In fact, some students find it easier to identify non-fiction genres than the standard fiction genres. Genres of non-fiction can be identified by one single factor: the intent, or purpose, of the writing. Genres of fiction blend together. A fantasy story can have characteristics of an adventure story, but not all adventure stories are fantasies. The difference between genres such as adventure and fantasy can be difficult for students to identify, since many components are used to create them.

....
In general, genres of non-fiction are more clearly defined than fiction. They explain the intent of the author or the purpose of the material.
....

The six main genres for non-fiction are:

1. instructional: using steps to describe how something is made
2. explanatory: telling what happened or how something works, with reasons
3. report: telling how things are
4. discussion: looking at both sides of an idea and making a decision
5. opinion: deciding on a point of view and having reasons to support the view
6. relate: retelling information or events for an audience

Language Structures Used in Genres of Non-Fiction

The following language chart provides information for students about the genres of non-fiction. The chart illustrates that most non-fiction is written in present tense, and that non-fiction does not follow the rule of chronological order in half the situations.

Genre	Tense	Sequence	Language
Instructional	present tense	chronological order	uses simplistic form of language or point form; uses verb clauses (do this, do that, etc.)
Explanatory	present tense	most often in chronological order but not necessary	temporal language (then, after, first, next, etc.); uses cause-and-effect words
Report	present tense	does not have to be in chronological order	summations occur regularly
Discussion	present tense	does not have to be in chronological order	comparisons and contrasting language
Opinion	present tense	does not have to be in chronological order	inferences used often
Relate	past tense	chronological order	verb clauses

The Other Genre of Non-Fiction: Blended Text

Although students will engage most often in these six main genres, another form of non-fiction has been gaining in popularity over the past few years. This is *blended text* or *Info fiction.*

Info fiction is a blended form of text that uses factual content and opinion to create a narrative storytelling form. Biographies and true crime stories will often use blended text, and it is a form of print students will encounter. Authors of Info fiction tell a story of fact using the narrative form. Authors rely on inferences to fill in details that may not be possible to obtain.

One of the most popular blended texts in the past few years has been the book *The Perfect Storm* by Sebastian Junger. In his book, Junger is able to use factual details to account for a ship and crew lost at sea in a storm. He has all the factual detail for the ship's sinking, but he lacks the personal narrative, such as the crew's reaction to their imminent deaths. Junger must infer what the crew was feeling in these last moments of their lives. This is blended text or Info fiction at work.

Blended text can be controversial. Some critics think the division between fact and fiction is too blurred. As a genre, it can be an excellent tool for teaching students inferring skills and how to distinguish between fact and opinion.

Blended text material is very conducive to novel studies and literature circles. Teachers can develop activities related to students' abilities to research. When reading blended text, students should develop a system for identifying facts, confirming them as fact, and verifying the validity of the information. These are skills that students will have to practise before they can become critical readers of Info fiction.

STRUCTURES OF NON-FICTION: THE FORMAT

As students begin to understand the different purposes of non-fiction, they must also become aware of the *structures* of non-fiction. An author wishing to create an opinion-based piece of non-fiction has several options for the format it may take. Some formats are more conducive to certain genres of non-fiction, while others may be applied to all genres. During small-group instruction, teachers guide the students to understand and identify these structures. Teachers attempt to expose students to as many different structures as possible in the school year, as well as use the same structure for different genres. Students begin to realize the author has choice in the format he/she wishes to use to express their message (intent/purpose).

Structures/Formats of Non-Fiction			
almanacs	editorials	magazine articles	presentations
autobiographies	essays	manuals	proposals
biographies	evaluations	newspaper articles	recipes
book/movie reviews	guides	notices	reports
brochures	interviews	obituaries	request forms
consumer reports	journals	observations	rules
debates	letters	polls/surveys	speeches
demonstrations	logs	postcards	travelogues

Students should be aware of the variety and makeup of structures of non-fiction. Some structures or formats of non-fiction lend themselves to a variety of genres. A speech can be instructional, explanatory, a report, opinion, discussion, or relating, while a recipe is solely instructional in nature. The structures can be categorized into the different genres, but there will always be variations—this is what helps to make non-fiction material unique and interesting. Students can become quite involved in discussions regarding categorization of structures. A structure can take on completely different tones and appearances, depending on the author's intent. As students become exposed to different structures with different purposes, they gain further knowledge of non-fiction.

Discussion

Biographies	Consumer Reports
Editorials	Essays
Evaluations	Magazine Articles
Observations	Presentations
Reports	Speeches
Summaries	Debates

Instructional

Brochures	Demonstrations
Guides	Letters
Manuals	Magazine Articles
Newspaper Articles	
Presentations	Recipes
Reports	Rules
Speeches	Logs

Report

Almanacs	Biographies
Brochures	Consumer Reports
Essays	Evaluations
Guides	Interviews
Journals	Letters
Logs	Magazine Articles
Manuals	Notices
Newspaper Articles	
Observations	Polls/Surveys
Postcards	Presentations
Reports	Speeches
Summaries	Travelogues

Opinion

Biographies	Book/Movie Reviews
Debates	Demonstrations
Editorials	Essays
Evaluations	Interviews
Journals	Letters
Logs	Magazine Articles
Observations	Postcards
Presentations	Proposals
Reports	Speeches
Request Forms	Summaries
Travelogues	

Structures in Different Genres of Non-Fiction

Relate

Almanacs	Autobiographies	Biographies
Brochures	Demonstrations	Essays
Guides	Interviews	Journals
Letters	Logs	Magazine Articles
Notices	Observations	Obituaries
Postcards	Presentations	Proposals
Reports	Request Forms	Speeches
Summaries	Travelogues	

Explanatory

Brochures	Consumer Reports
Demonstrations	Essays
Letters	Magazine Articles
Manuals	Observations
Newspaper Articles	Presentations
Request Forms	Reports
Speeches	Summaries
Guides	

NON-FICTION STYLE: TECHNIQUES/STRATEGIES

Non-fiction readers use the same techniques and strategies that writers implement in the writing. All forms of writing rely on techniques and strategies. In fiction, author O. Henry was well known for his use of irony, and Edgar Allan Poe used setting to present his many images of darkness. Non-fiction writers use different techniques to convey their purpose/intent. Students should be able to recognize these techniques in a piece of non-fiction material. The tone of a non-fiction piece will vary, depending on the *style* an author adopts. A report will have a different makeup if the author chooses to summarize information rather than develop inferences from which a reader can draw conclusions. Authors use these techniques in the writing, and the reader applies an understanding of the techniques during the reading process, making them important reading strategies.

Styles/Strategies in Non-Fiction Material

Writers of non-fiction use the following styles/strategies in their work:

- developing cause-and-effect relationships
- comparing and contrasting
- sequencing
- summarizing and paraphrasing
- inferring and drawing conclusions
- classifying and categorizing data
- distinguishing fact from opinion
- identifying main ideas and supporting details

The reader of non-fiction uses these same styles to analyze the material. When students apply the strategies to non-fiction text, they are able to develop a stronger sense of the intent of the material and thus retain more information regarding the content. These strategies are used in conjunction with the students' existing knowledge of reading techniques, such as predicting, word analysis, and comprehension.

The following chart illustrates the relationship between the author and reader of non-fiction.

Author Creates		**Reader Looks For**
• Cause-and-effect relationships		• Cause-and-effect relationships
• Comparisons and contrasting of ideas		• Comparisons and contrasting ideas
• Sequence of ideas		• Sequencing of ideas
• Summaries and paraphrased ideas		• Summaries and paraphrased ideas
• Inferences and conclusions		• Inferences and conclusions
• A system of classification and categories for data		• A system of classification and categorization of data
• A structure using fact or opinion, or a blending		• Use of fact or opinion, or a blending
• Main ideas with supporting details		• Main ideas with supporting details

Styles of Non-Fiction Defined

Developing Cause-and-Effect Relationships
- This is a way to organize non-fiction that discusses why a particular event happened and the consequences of that particular event.
- A *cause* makes something happen; an *effect* is what happens as a result of that cause.
- Specific words show the cause-and effect relationship; for example, *accordingly, because, in order that,* and *since.*

Comparing and Contrasting
- This is a way to organize non-fiction that details similarities and differences between subjects.
- Comparison and contrast are two thought processes used on a daily basis.
- When we compare two things, we show how they are similar; when we contrast two things, we show how they are different.

Sequencing
- This is the organization of the order of events in an informational piece.
- Non-fiction material can be sequenced in many ways; for example, paragraphs can be written in chronological order, written in a sequence of importance, or can provide a list.

Summarizing/Paraphrasing
- This means restating the author's ideas in our own words.
- When we summarize, we retell the original material in our own words to convey the main ideas.

- When we paraphrase, we rewrite the material in our own words, keeping the essence of the original ideas.

Inferring and Drawing Conclusions
- This means using existing knowledge to discover something new.
- Inferential thinking is reading "between the lines" and determining the intent.
- Drawing conclusions involves the process of collecting data, analyzing it, and generating ideas based on the data.

Classifying and Categorizing
- These are essential skills for organizing information into logical and usable groups of data.
- These are especially helpful for separating important from unimportant information, one of the main skills of effective reading.
- Categorizing depends on our ability to analyze data.

Distinguishing Fact from Opinion
- A *fact* is a statement that can be proven. A fact can be checked for accuracy.
- An *opinion* is a statement of a belief or a judgment that cannot be proven true or false.
- Opinions usually express the feelings or preferences of a person about a topic.
- A fact is not the opposite of an opinion. A fact is a type of statement.
- If a fact is untrue or false, it does not necessarily become an opinion. In the same way, even if an opinion is believed by a majority, it does not necessarily become a fact.

Identifying Main Ideas and Supporting Details
- A *paragraph* is a group of sentences related to a particular topic or central theme. Every paragraph has a key concept or main idea.
- The main idea is the important piece of information the author wants us to know.
- Details, major and minor, support the main idea by telling how, what, when, where, why, how much, or how many.
- Locating the main idea and supporting details helps us understand the point(s) the writer is attempting to express.

ELEMENTS OF NON-FICTION: FEATURES

Non-fiction material can integrate many different forms of print: graphic forms such as charts, pictures, and graphs; structural forms such as glossaries, indexes, and guide words; and physical appearance such as bold print, italics, and varying fonts. The use of many different *elements* creates a unique presentation of the material.

The features can be:

- effective tools for the author to convey the intent and for the reader to discuss the intent or purpose of the text;
- numerous and varied, with several different ones applied to a single piece of non-fiction; and
- a source of additional information, separate from the main text.

Many inexperienced readers have difficulty using features of non-fiction in an effective manner. Students will often ignore these features, believing that only the traditional form of text will give the information they need. As part of small-group instruction, teachers should guide students towards these features and show them how to use them effectively.

The following are elements or features of non-fiction:

- bold print
- charts
- captions
- diagrams
- flow charts
- footnotes
- fonts
- glossaries
- graphs
- guide words
- headings/subheadings
- indexes
- italicized words
- labels
- maps
- pictures
- pronunciation guides
- sidebars
- table of contents
- timelines

Elements in non-fiction help us locate and understand information. Not all features are used in all types of non-fiction. Some features are better suited to books rather than articles, which are usually shorter and more specific. Some features may be used in both forms of non-fiction.

Features Suited to Book Form
glossaries   guide words   indexes   tables of contents

Features Suited to Book and Article Form
bold print   charts   captions   diagrams   flow charts   footnotes   fonts   graphs headings/subheadings   italicized words   labels   maps   pictures   pronunciation guides   sidebars   timelines

Non-fiction writers will use multiple elements, or features, in one piece. Some features are more conducive to certain structures, while others are more universal. Bold print can be found in any structure, but a table of contents is effective for longer pieces of non-fiction, rather than for a magazine article. Authors will use features to include additional information on their topic, not found in the main text, or to reinforce an idea already stated. Often, inexperienced readers of non-fiction are under the false assumption that these features contain redundant information and ignore them for this reason. Teachers need to guide students toward the understanding that features may add new information or enhance existing information.

Elements/Features Defined

Bold Print   Text printed in a darker tone than the surrounding print. Letters are often thicker and larger. Used to emphasize word(s).

Captions   One or two sentences that describe an illustration or photograph. Usually appear underneath the picture but can also be above or to the side.

Chart   A defined space (often a box) presenting information in the form of graphs or lists.

Diagram   A plan, sketch, drawing, or outline to show or explain how something works or to explain the relationship among the parts of a whole.

Flow Chart   An organized combination of shapes, lines, and text that pictorially illustrates a series of steps, a process, or structure.

Font	A complete set of type of one size and appearance. Can be different styles, sizes, and colours. Often used to highlight important information.
Footnote	A note placed at the bottom of a page of a piece of writing that comments on, or recognizes, another text.
Glossary	A small dictionary that contains words from the non-fiction piece you are reading. Usually found at the end of the work.
Graph	A diagram or picture that shows a relationship between two sets of numbers or a quantity. Different types include plot, stem graph, pie chart, or bar graph.
Guide Words	Words that appear in bold print at the top of glossary or dictionary pages and indicate the other words that will be listed on that particular page.
Headings/ Subheadings	Headings are usually found at the top of the page or paragraph, in a larger or coloured font. They describe the topic or paragraph in a one- or two-word phrase. Subheadings appear within the text.
Index	An alphabetical list of all the subjects in a non-fiction book. Found at the back of a book.
Italicized Word	A style of printing type with the letters slanting to the right. Used to bring attention to a specific word, phrase, or title.
Label/Caption	Usually added to photographs or illustrations to provide more information. Often define or name an object.
Map	A representation, usually on a flat surface, of all or part of the earth or some other geographical body, showing a group of features and their relationship to size and position and place.
Picture	A visual piece of information (photographic or illustrated). Adds further information to the text.
Pronunciation Guide	A graphic representation of the way a word is spoken, using phonetic symbols.
Sidebar	Information on the side of the page. Provides text or illustrations that add details to the main topic.
Table of Contents	A list of all the chapters in a book, found at the beginning of a book.
Timeline	A type of graphic organizer that arranges information by chronological order (time).

CHAPTER TWO

STUDENTS AND THE READING PROCESS

The pioneering research of Don Holdaway, in his book *The Foundations of Literacy* (1984), provides valuable information in determining the purpose of small-group instruction. Holdaway states there are four processes that allow students to acquire reading ability.

- The first process is *observation* of reading behaviours, which includes being read to and observing teachers modelling reading strategies. Holdaway's first process is the basis for adapting a guided reading approach towards small-group instruction focusing on non-fiction.
- The second process is *collaboration,* referred to as the interaction with peers and adults related to reading. Holdaway's second process reinforces the belief in the value of small-group instruction.
- The third process is *practice,* where the learner independently tries out what has been taught. Holdaway's third process helps the teacher apply management to the program.
- The fourth and final process is *performance,* in which the students share what they have learned, and create a product. Holdaway's fourth process helps the teacher apply management to the program.

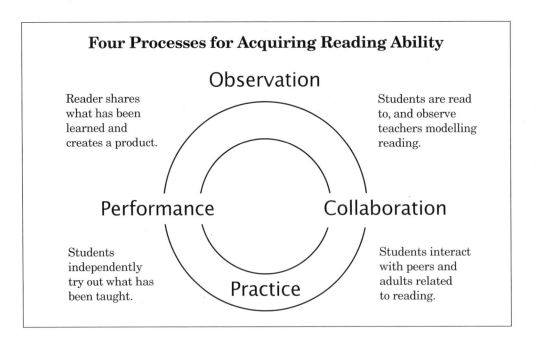

Four Processes for Acquiring Reading Ability

Observation

Reader shares what has been learned and creates a product.

Students are read to, and observe teachers modelling reading.

Performance

Collaboration

Students independently try out what has been taught.

Students interact with peers and adults related to reading.

Practice

THE FIRST PROCESS—OBSERVATION
Providing Students with Models for Reading

Small-group instruction periods provide many opportunities for the teacher to model successful reading strategies with non-fiction material. The teacher can model the methods for using features of non-fiction, such as examining maps and graphs to gain more meaning from the print. Teacher-directed questions can lead students towards learning how to become efficient readers of non-fiction.

The key element in Holdaway's first process, *observation*, is modelling reading behaviours for students. Fundamental reading behaviours are not established with all students. Each student has their own unique experiences with reading. The teacher can assess the students' abilities and create small groups based on specific needs.

An example of a specific need may be with students who experience difficulty in self-selecting material for reading. A handout, such as the following "How to Select a Book," can be the basis for a small-group discussion. The handout offers students who are visual learners an opportunity to engage in the suggested behaviours along with the oral learners who gain knowledge · from the discussion group.

As the handout is discussed, the teacher can provide examples of non-fiction material and demonstrate the process of reviewing a book to ensure it will fit the needs of the reader. This is an important skill for students to have, especially with non-fiction material. Students will encounter many different sources of material on the same subject. It is important for students to learn how to self-select material appropriate for their level of understanding. This also becomes a foundation for students when they begin research projects.

How to Select a Book

When you decide to read a book, you want to make sure you have picked a book that will be right for you. Selecting a book is similar to shopping for clothes. You don't want to pick the first thing and then find out it doesn't fit you. Just like clothes, not all books are for everyone. Each person's choice of books is suited just for them. Here are some tips that can help you make that important decision—how to select a book that's just right for you.

Readability of Book   Can you understand the ideas and words in the book?

Subject of Book   Is the subject something you are interested in or want to know more about?

Description of Book   Does the description on the back or inside cover make you want to look inside for more information?

Interesting Cover and Illustrations   When you look at the cover or pictures inside, do they make you want to find out more about the book?

Author's Reputation   Is the author one you know or one whose work you have read before? Do you think you would enjoy their writing?

Title of Book   Does the title sound interesting to you and make you curious about what is inside the book?

Think of yourself as a wise shopper when making a book choice. When people purchase a car, they test-drive it before they decide if they want to buy it. It is similar with books. Once you have asked yourself some of these questions, test-read the book. Read the first couple of pages before you decide on your selection. If you find the first few pages hold your interest, then you may have found a book that's just right for you.

THE SECOND PROCESS—COLLABORATION
Building a Community of Readers

Collaboration, Holdway's second process, is the interaction of students with peers and adults related to the subject of reading, and works naturally for small-group instruction. The small group is conducive to a setting in which students feel safe to take risks with their reading, to gain new knowledge of reading strategies, and to acquire new information. Students can also use the collaborative process in a large-group setting when the teacher chooses material for reading aloud. Read-aloud sessions are an opportune time to share non-fiction material with students and stimulate group discussions. The large-group discussions, combined with small-group instruction, help to develop community, which is the fundamental principle behind collaboration.

Non-Fiction Bibliography

Many classrooms have self-contained libraries with a variety of books. A balanced classroom library would have equal amounts of fiction and non-fiction for readers. School and local libraries can also be a source for materials.

It is important to remember that non-fiction does not have to be in a book form. There are many valuable magazines available as well as local newspapers. The following are suggestions for books and magazines for a classroom library. The compiled titles are suitable for grades four to seven.

Non-Fiction Books and Magazines for the Classroom

Biography (Discussion)
Jump! From the Life of Michael Jordan by Floyd Cooper (Philonel Books 2004)
Leonardo, Beautiful Dreamer by Robert Byrd (Penguin 2003)
Odd Boy Out: Young Albert Einstein by Don Brown (Houghton Mifflin 2004)
Shipwrecked! The True Adventures of a Japanese Boy by Rhoda Blumberg
   (Harper Collins 2001)
The Boy on Fairfield Street: How Ted Geisel Grew Up to Become Dr. Seuss by
   Kathleen Krill (Random House 2004)

Instructional
The Art Book for Children by the editors of Phaidon Press (Phaidon Press 2005)
Brain Juice: Science Freshly Squeezed by Carol Diggory Shields (Handprint
   Books 2003)
Drawing Mammals by Darcy Lindstrand (Fox Chapel Publishing 2001)
Knitting by Judy Ann Sadler (Kids Can Press 2002)
The Never Bored Kids Book by Joy Evans and Jo Ellen Moore (Evan-Moor 2003)
Puppy Training for Kids by Sarah Whitehead (Barron's Educational Series 2001)

Historical

1000 Years Ago on Planet Earth by Sneed B. Collard III (Houghton Mifflin 1999)

How Sweet It Is (and Was): The History of Candy by Ruth Freeman Swan (Holiday 2003)

Science in Ancient Egypt by Geraldine Woods (Franklin Watts 1998)

Turn of the Century by Ellen Jackson (Charlesbridge Press 1998)

Earth Sciences

The Best Book of Fossils, Rocks, and Minerals by Chris Perrault (Kingfisher 2000)

Earthquakes by Seymour Simon (Mulberry Books 1995)

Earth from Above for Young Readers by Robert Burleigh (Abrams 2002)

Animals

Black Bear: North America's Bear by Stephen R. Swinburne (Boyds Mills Press 2003)

Exploding Ants: Amazing Facts About How Animals Adapt by Joanne Settel (Atheneum 1999)

The Kids' Horse Book by Sylvia Funston (Mapletree Press 2004)

The Mysteries of Animal Intelligence: True Stories of Animals with Amazing Abilities by Brad and Mary Steiger (Tor Books 1995)

Whales! Strange and Wonderful by Laurence Pringle (Boyds Mills Press 2003)

Geography

Destination Antarctica by Robert Swan (Scholastic 1999)

G'Day Australia! (Our Amazing Continents) by April Pulley Sayre (Millbrook Press 2003)

North America (Rookie Read-About Geography) by Alan Fowler (Children's Press 2001)

The New York Public Library Amazing World Geography: A Book of Answers for Kids by Andrea Sutcliffe (Jossey-Bass 2002)

On Top of the World: The Conquest of Mount Everest by Mary Ann Fraser (Henry Holt 1991)

Report

All Aboard!: Passenger Trains Around the World by Karl Zimmermann (Boyds Mills Press 2006)

Amazing Dinosaurs: The Fiercest, the Tallest, the Toughest, the Smallest by Dougal Dixon (Boyds Mills Press 2000)

Coin Collecting for Kids by Steve Otfinoski (Innovative Kids 2000)

Hottest Coldest Highest Deepest by Steve Jenkins (Houghton Mifflin 1998)

It's Disgusting and We Ate It! True Food Facts from Around the World and Throughout History by James Solheim (Aladdin 2001)

I Want to Be a Fashion Designer by Stephanie Maze (Harcourt Books 2000)

Oh, Yuck: The Encyclopedia of Everything Nasty by Joy Masoff (Workman Publishing Co. 2000)

The Story of Valentine's Day by Clyde Robert Bulla (Harper Trophy 2000)

Relating

Dirt Track Racing (Motorcycles) by Ed Youngblood (Capstone Press 2000)

The Girls' Book of Wisdom: Empowering, Inspirational Quotes from Over 400 Fabulous Females by Catherine Dee (Megan Tingley Books 1999)

Flying Machine (DK Eyewitness Books) by DK Publishing (DK Children 2004)

Olympics—Eyewitness Books by DK Publishing (DK Children 2005)

Number Four, Bobby Orr! by Mike Leonetti (Raincoast Books 2003)

The Hockey Book for Girls by Stacy Wilson (Kids Can Press 2000)

Why Does a Ball Bounce? 101 Questions You Never Thought of Asking by Adam Hart Davis (Firefly Books 2005)

Opinion

Incredible You! 10 Ways to Be Happy Inside and Out by Wayne Dyer (Hay House 2005)

My Life with the Chimpanzees by Jane Goodall (Aladdin 1996)

Explanatory

Cool Stuff and How It Works by Chris Woodford (DK Children 2005)

Kids' Magic Card Tricks by Terry Eagle (Barron's Educational Series 2003)

The Reasons for Seasons by Gail Gibbons (Holiday House 1996)

Why Frogs Are Wet by Judy Hawes (Harper Trophy 2000)

Discussion

Lives of Extraordinary Women: Rulers, Rebels (And What the Neighbors Thought) by Kathleen Krull (Harcourt 2000)

Spirit of Endurance: The True Story of the Shackleton Expedition to the Antarctic by Jennifer Armstrong (Crown 2000)

Magazines

Boys' Life

Children's Digest

Click Magazine

Dig Magazine

Discovery Girls Magazine

Girls' Life

Highlights Magazine

Kids World

Kids Discover

National Geographic Kids
Owl Magazine
Ranger Rick
Sports Illustrated for Kids
Think and Discover Magazine
Your Big Backyard

THE THIRD PROCESS—PRACTICE
Creating Opportunities for Students to Show What They Know
Reading Record and Letter Writing

The Reading Record letter to the teacher is a principle of the third process, *practice*. Each week students write a letter about their reading from that week. The letter may reflect upon a specific book they are reading or a letter about themselves as a reader. The Reading Record letter allows students the opportunity to create a product and demonstrate the knowledge they have learned. It also becomes a form of assessment for teachers.

Some letters can be written to other students in the class and some letters handed in to the teacher to read. On any given day, the teacher may have four or five students turn in their letters and have the remaining letters distributed to other class members. The receiver then responds to the letter. This system helps students take time to reflect on their reading, as well as builds the community atmosphere of readers.

Early in the year, teachers can provide students with a structure for writing a response letter and can share samples. In addition to this, teachers should explain the rubric they use for assessment. This is part of a "feedback for learning" philosophy for the students.

While the students may use the Reading Record for all their reading throughout the year, the activity takes on the specific function of recording and reflecting on non-fiction during the periods scheduled for small-group instruction related to non-fiction material.

The following pages provide charts and handouts for students and teachers. The material includes sample reading records, guides to rating books, an assessment rubric, and response journal records. These may be adapted as necessary.

Reading Record

Title/Author	Date Completed	Pages	Rating

A Reading Record

Your Reading Record will be a place for you and me as well as other readers to talk about books, authors, reading, and writing. You will be chatting about books in letters to me and other interested readers, and we will write back to you. All our letters will stay here together as a record of our thoughts, learning, and the reading we do together.

In your letters, talk about what you have read. Tell me what you thought and felt, and why. Tell me what you liked and didn't like, and why. Ask questions or ask for help. Tell what these books said, and what they meant to you, and I'll write back my ideas, feelings, and questions.

When you finish a letter, hand over your Reading Record to the person you wish to share with and let them write back in your Record. If you should receive someone's Reading Record, make sure to take care of it and return it to them as soon as possible.

In addition to letter writing, your Reading Record is a place where you can keep track of the books you read throughout the year. Every time you finish a book, fill in a section of the information pages right away before you forget any important details. This record will help you look back later to all the books you have been involved with throughout the year.

I can't wait for your letters and I am anxious to hear from you about the many different books that you end up reading this year.

Your teacher,

Rating Books

This year you will be reading many different books. Some of the stories you read will become real favourites of yours. At other times, you may read a book but not be sure how you feel about it. Because you will be reading so many books this year, it can become easy to forget your opinions on a story, especially if a long time passes before you write your response. Rating a book will give you a record of your feelings about a book right after you finish it. This gives you a chance to look back on your reading and review your opinions. Here is a rating system we will be using in our class this year.

* * * *   Excellent

This is a book that becomes one of your all-time favourites. You still think about it even though you have finished it. When you were reading it, you couldn't put it down. You would recommend this book to others.

* * *   Good

When you were reading this book, you found it to be enjoyable. If someone asked you about it, you would tell them to take the time to read it.

* *   Fair

You are still not sure about this book, even after finishing it. There were some parts of the book that you thought were really good, yet there were parts you did not like.

*   Poor

You managed to get through the book but it was hard to do. The book may be good for someone else, but it was not right for you. You would tell people what you did not like about it if you were asked.

Reading Record Letters

Books give readers stories and information. The books people read and enjoy help to remind them of events that have happened in their lives or things that they have seen or heard about. Books can help readers learn new information. Finally, books make readers think. They make them wonder about new ideas or thoughts.

This year, you and your classmates will be writing Reading Record letters.

A Reading Record letter contains these three parts: a short retelling of what was read; a part relating new information or connecting the story to your life; and a part reflecting on, or thinking about, what the story or information means to you. When you write a Reading Record letter, include at least one paragraph on each of the following:

Retell

Tell about the subject you are reading. Explain the main events or information. Tell about your favourite parts of the book.

Relate or Connect

Describe a memory of something that has happened to you, related to the book. Tell how the information in the book is important to you. Explain how the book is similar to another one you have read.

Reflect

Think about what you have read. Does the book make you have questions? Have you become curious about something? Did the book help you understand an idea?

Sample Reading Record Letter

Dear Mr. Rossi,

    I just want to tell you a little bit about the book I just finished reading. It is called *The Kids' Book of Soccer* and it is written by Brooks Clark. It was really helpful to me.

Retell

    In the book all the rules to soccer are explained and they were easy to understand and remember but the book also has more, which makes it so good. It tells you the different positions, shows you the different kinds of kicks you can make. I liked how the book had diagrams to show you where to move on the field.

Relate

    The reason I decided to read this book is because I want to join the school soccer team that plays at lunch time but I was kind of embarrassed about not knowing the rules and was too shy to ask anyone. So I decided I'd learn the rules from a book and I did! I think I am ready to try to join one of the teams.

Reflect

    In the book, I learned you can turn to the index and look up different rules and it tells you what page they are on. This is good because if I forget a rule, all I have to do is turn to the back of the book and look up the rule. If this works out okay, I think I might find a book on football and try to learn the rules for that game too. Football is another sport I'm not too sure how to play but now that I know you can find out the rules in a book, maybe it won't be so hard to join sports teams in the future.

    From your future soccer player,

Response Journal Records

Student Name	Date	Retells 1–3	Relates 1–3	Reflects 1–3

Response Journal Rubric

	1	2	3
Retell	Provides limited information; able to recall isolated facts and details	Is able to give general overview of material	Provides comprehensive synopsis, relevant information related to central themes
Relate	Makes very few connections	Is able to connect to some actions/events in story	Is able to apply own experiences to themes and characters in story
Reflect	Expresses limited opinions, a basic like or dislike of material	Is able to explain some central themes; has opinions/questions	Has a good understanding of main themes; able to extend ideas beyond book; draws conclusions

THE FOURTH PROCESS—PERFORMANCE

Engaging Students with Non-Fiction

In order for students to become skilled with non-fiction print, teachers must extend the learning process. They must create situations for students to demonstrate their knowledge. This relates to Holdaway's fourth process of reading instruction, *performance*. During small-group instruction times, the teacher may have the other students involved in performance activities connected to non-fiction.

Students may be involved in creating their own structures of non-fiction, using the information they have learned from their personal reading. Some suggestions are:

- book reviews;
- instructions for a new game;
- a research project based on a theme of their own choosing;
- a student-related quiz; or
- a set of postcards from a country they have studied.

At other times, students may be working with a specific piece of non-fiction and applying strategies of non-fiction style to generate further meaning. Some of the options that can help students become more proficient with reading strategies for non-fiction are:

- doing an activity related to cause-and-effect process in an article;
- writing a summary based on a report; or
- using a graphic organizer to classify and categorize information from an article.

CHAPTER THREE

THE LESSONS

MINI-LESSONS TO ACTIVATE THOUGHT

In order for students to engage in non-fiction material, there must be some "activating thought." The mini-lessons in this chapter will help to activate student thinking by giving students background information to proceed to other non-fiction reading. Resources are provided as sample activating mini-lessons. Teachers have options for the method they wish to use for the mini-lessons. They can be used as reading mini-lessons, involving the whole class, or they can be used in the small-group situation. Most teachers tend to use them as a whole-group mini-lesson, since they are related to information with which they want all students to be familiar. If some students are struggling with the concepts of the mini-lesson, they may join the small group and work with a set of students needing the same attention. Teachers should modify the activating mini-lessons when necessary to help these students develop an understanding of the concepts.

All the activities are based on the four main components of non-fiction:
1. **genre** (purpose or intent)
2. **structure** (the format used)
3. **style** (techniques and strategies applied)
4. **element** (features used to convey the message)

The mini-lessons compiled in each section work towards activating thoughts on the four main components of non-fiction. The following is a summary of the organization of the mini-lessons.

1. Mini-Lessons to Activate *Genre* (purpose or intent)
- What Is Non-Fiction?
- Classifying and Categorizing Non-Fiction
- Using Non-Fiction Every Day

2. Mini-Lessons to Activate *Structure* (format used)
- Introducing Different Structures
- Finding the Right Piece of Non-Fiction

3. Mini-Lessons to Activate *Style* (techniques and strategies applied)
- Using Background Information
- Using Inferences
- Learning New Vocabulary
- Remembering Important Details—Main Idea and Supporting Details
- Drawing Conclusions from What You Read
- Distinguishing Fact from Opinion

4. Mini-Lessons to Activate *Elements* (features used to convey the message)
- The Importance of Graphs
- Table of Contents
- Finding Elements in Non-Fiction

1. MINI-LESSONS TO ACTIVATE *GENRE*

The activating lessons provided here are designed to offer students background information about the six main genres of non-fiction.

1.1 Mini-Lesson: What Is Non-Fiction?

Non-Fiction Component: _X_ Genre   ___Structure   ___Style   ___Element

Process: _X_ Observation   ___Collaboration   ___Practice   ___Performance

Set-Up: ___Individual   ___Small Group   _X_ Whole Class

Goal: Students become aware of the intent or purpose of non-fiction. Students develop a more comprehensive view of non-fiction, rather than viewing it as the opposite of fiction or as solely regulated to basic facts.

Materials Required: Chart: What Is Non-Fiction?

Procedure: The tree diagram provided serves as a starting point for a discussion about non-fiction. Even with the definition of terms for the six main genres of non-fiction, students will not grasp these concepts until they are provided with concrete examples. It is through identifying and continued use of the concepts that students will eventually be able to label different structures of non-fiction based on their genre. When this occurs, students will have developed a deeper comprehension of non-fiction.

Assessment: Teachers make ongoing classroom observations/anecdotal notes on student attitudes to non-fiction.

Extension Activity: Take the students into the school or public library to survey the available non-fiction resources.

What Is Non-Fiction?

It is understanding something from our world. It can help us do things.

It is information that is believed to be true.

It is written by an author who has a purpose.

Deciding on an opinion and having reasons to prove the point of view.

This is called **Opinion.**

Telling what happened or how something works and providing reasons.

This is called **Explanatory.**

Using steps to describe how something is made.

This is called **Instructional.**

Retelling information or events for an audience.

This is called **Relating.**

Looking at both sides of an idea and making a decision.

This is called **Discussion.**

Telling how things are.

This is called a **Report.**

1.2 Mini-Lesson: Classifying and Categorizing Non-Fiction

Non-Fiction Component: _X_ Genre ___Structure ___Style ___Element

Process: ___Observation _X_ Collaboration ___Practice ___Performance

Set-Up: ___Individual _X_ Small Group ___Whole Class

Goal: Students are able to classify pieces of non-fiction according to genre and attach the correct label to each piece of work.

Materials Required: Classifying Non-Fiction Genres Activity Sheet; six sample sheets

Procedure: Groups are provided with six short samples of reading material. The students may read them as a group, one at a time, out loud to each other, or independently, circulating the samples among the group. As a group, the students classify each piece according to its genre and attach the correct label to each piece of work. This activity often stimulates discussion. Students come to realize that within some of the genres, there is overlapping of purpose, while others are more clearly distinct. Students most often identify instructional material immediately because of the elements used in it, whereas relating and reporting are often difficult to distinguish and require repeated exposure before students can determine the fine, yet important, differences.

Assessment: Students demonstrate ability to classify genre according to recognized criteria. The students' performance on the activity sheet will help teachers determine if students are developing an understanding of the concepts.

Extension Activity: Students can create pieces of non-fiction using the same topic but in different genres. For example, students create different genres of writing on the topic of UFOs. Possible pieces could be:

> Instructional: How to Search the Night Sky for UFOs
> Opinion: UFOs—More Fiction than Fact
> Discussion: Could There Be Such a Thing as UFOs?
> Report: Man Claims to See UFO
> Explanatory: Why So Many UFO Sightings Are Mistakes
> Relate: UFO Club Keeps Watch of Night Sky

When students share these different pieces of writing, they see a dramatic illustration of the different forms a piece of non-fiction can take when the intent or purpose shifts.

Classifying Non-Fiction Genres Activity Sheet

Non-fiction is not all the same. There are different types based on what the author is trying to do (this is called the "author's purpose"). Read the following six samples of non-fiction and decide by which genre of non-fiction each sample should be labelled.

Telling how things are.
This is called a **Report.**

SAMPLE #

_____

Using steps to describe
how something is made.
This is called **Instructional.**

SAMPLE #

_____

Deciding on an opinion
and having reasons to
prove the point of view.
This is called **Opinion.**

SAMPLE #

_____

Looking at both sides of an
idea and making a decision.
This is called **Discussion.**

SAMPLE #

_____

Retelling information or
events for an audience.
This is called **Relating.**

SAMPLE #

_____

Telling what happened or
how something works and
providing reasons. This is
called **Explanatory.**

SAMPLE #

_____

SAMPLE # 1

Making Slime!

Is it a solid? Is it a liquid? Make your very own slime and test it out!

You will need the following materials:
- spoon
- 1 teaspoon (5 ml) of white school glue
- 1 teaspoon (5 ml) liquid starch
- 1 drop food colouring
- 30 cm square sheet of waxed paper
- timer

Steps

1. Using a spoon, mix the starch, the glue, and the drop of food colouring on the waxed paper. Keep stirring the ingredients until the material starts to separate from the paper.
2. Let the new material stand on the waxed paper for three to four minutes. Use your timer to keep track of time.
3. Roll the mixture into a ball with your hands for about one minute. You should then have your slime!

Test It Out!

See what you can do with your slime. Does it bounce? Pull on it. Does it stretch? What else do you notice about it?

SAMPLE # 2

A SHOCK FOR ELDERLY WOMAN

Police in the small town of Weeble were surprised by a recent call about an intruder in a home. The shocking part for police was the type of intruder.

Mrs. Robbi of Wood Cove Road had left her house Saturday afternoon for her weekly trip to her hairdressing appointment. She estimated she was gone from her home for two hours.

On her return, as soon as she walked up her sidewalk, Mrs. Robbi knew something was wrong. The front door of her place was wide open and hanging from its hinges. Fearing burglars, Mrs. Robbi was about to head to her neighbour's and call the police when she noticed something unusual that made her turn around and go back to the house. Muddy footprints were covering her doormat but they did not look like a person's steps.

Curiosity got the better of Mrs. Robbi and she entered her home. She followed the muddy prints until she heard a strange sound coming from the kitchen. It was the sound of birds chirping, along with a low growling noise.

Mrs. Robbi poked her head through the swinging door of the kitchen and found a bear sitting on the floor with its paw in the freshly baked pie she had made just before she left.

The bear was eating away while the birds were sitting on the table, pecking at crumbs.

Mrs. Robbi quickly ran to her neighbour's place to call the police.

When the police arrived, they had to call Animal Services to help remove the bear and the birds. Upon inspecting the house, the police discovered that the lock on Mrs. Robbi's front door had rusted away enough for the bear to enter easily and have some feathered friends follow along. Mrs. Robbi had left the pie to cool on the sill of an open window and the aroma was strong enough to attract the bear's attention.

SAMPLE # 3

HARRY POTTER AND THE HALF-BLOOD PRINCE
Is it as good as they say?

Harry Potter and the Half-Blood Prince by J.K. Rowling is the sixth book in the series and the best one so far.

The book has 652 pages and with each page you read, the further you will be on the edge of your seat, it is that exciting. There is adventure, some romance, and many more surprises that make it the kind of book that you simply must read.

Harry is sixteen now and there is only one year left before he comes of age and he is making more mature decisions. In the book, Harry learns more about the past of his greatest enemy, Lord Voldermort. He faces many other dangers. Harry returns to Hogwarts. He does not have a potions book and he is loaned one. This book has a lot of scribbling on it and makes it hard to read. Harry decides to try what the book says in the scribbling and it helps him. Then later, Harry looks at the cover and in very faint writing sees nine words:

"This Book is Property of The Half Blood Prince." This leads Harry to another mystery and adventure. But if you want to know more, then you'll just have to read the book for yourself. I'll say that I highly recommend it. Run to get your copy, if you don't already have one, and share the magic. Is it as good as people say? Most definitely!

How a Tadpole Becomes a Frog

In early spring, adult frogs wake up from their long winter sleep and start making their way to pools. Some frogs can travel very far to reach a pond. When the frogs reach the pond, breeding begins. The male croaks loudly to attract the female. As soon as the female releases her eggs into the water, they are fertilized by the male.

The eggs, or frogspawn, are surrounded by jelly, which floats to the surface of the pond, where the sun warms it. One clump of frogspawn can contain up to 4000 eggs. After about 10 days, a tadpole wriggles out of each egg.

At first the tadpole breathes and moves like a fish, using its gills and long tail, but after about five weeks the gills disappear and the tadpole develops lungs. It then has to swim to the surface of the water to gulp air. When a tadpole turns into a frog, the tadpole is going through a metamorphosis. *Metamorphosis* is a scientific word. *Meta* means 'change' and *morph* means 'shape.'

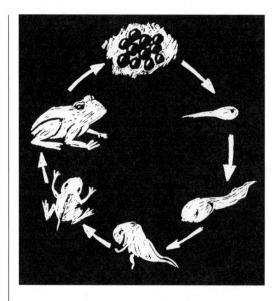

The tadpole transforms into a froglet, a small adult frog with four legs, no gills, and no tail. This takes about 8 to 11 weeks. At 12 to 14 weeks, the tail disappears and the tiny froglet is ready to leave the water. It will take three years before the froglet reaches maturity and the cycle starts all over again.

SAMPLE # 5

Is Pizza Junk Food?

We know that fast foods from some restaurants are not good for us. French fries and greasy burgers can lead to our being overweight and cause problems with our health when we grow up. What about pizza? Is it considered a fast food, junk food? Let us look more closely at pizza.

Large quantities of cheese and meat can be very fatty. Some pizzas spread oil on the dough when it is being cooked. It sounds as if pizza can be a very fattening food. In fact, pizza from fast-food restaurants contains large amounts of fat that are not healthy.

But recently, doctors are suggesting that pizza can be good for you! Scientists completed a four-year study that found that eating pizza can reduce your risk of a heart attack. They studied 1000 Italian people for their experiment. Italians are famous for their homemade pizzas. Those who ate pizza at least once a week were 30 percent less likely to experience a heart attack than those who didn't eat pizza.

But before you go running out for a pizza, there are some facts to know. The

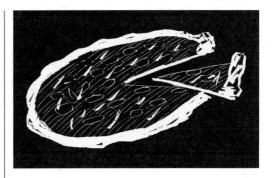

pizza eaten by the subjects in the study was homemade and did not contain as much fatty grease and meat as those found in fast-food restaurants. Homemade pizza contained less cheese, which is also high in fat. The study also found that the Italian eaters were more likely to use healthy toppings, such as vegetables, on homemade pizzas.

So, is pizza healthy for you? Well, it does contain four main food groups and, if the studies are correct, then it cannot hurt if it is eaten in the correct manner. Too much of any food is not good for you, but the occasional homemade pizza may be just what the doctor ordered. Bite into it!

SAMPLE # 6

HOW A PINBALL MACHINE WORKS

Since the first pinball game was released in 1947, people have enjoyed the game of pinball. The goals of the game are to score points and keep the pinball from going down the drain. In this article, we'll look at how pinball machines work.

The main parts of the game are the flippers and the pinball. The **flippers** are usually located at the bottom of the playfield, directly above the **drain**. One purpose of the flippers is to keep the pinball out of the drain. The other purpose is to propel the ball up the table toward the **bumpers** and **ramps** in order to score points—at times, extra flippers are placed farther up on the table for this purpose. The flippers are controlled with two buttons, one on either side of the machine, just below the table's top glass. The left button controls any and all flippers on the left side of the table, and the right button controls the ones on the right side.

The pinball moves around the table, hitting bumpers and **targets** to score. Otherwise, the ball falls down the drain and you move on to your next ball. You only get three balls. When your third ball goes down the drain, your game is over.

The back box of the table has two purposes: to hold the electronics of the game and to attract players with artwork located on the back glass. The bumpers and flippers are all tied into the main controller board located on the back

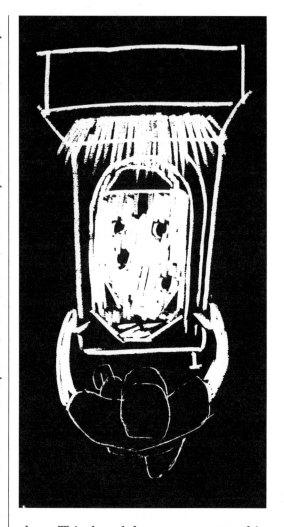

glass. This board has a computer chip that contains the information needed to play the game. The **wiring** runs from the controller board to the rest of the machine. These wires carry commands back and forth between the main board and the flippers, bumpers, targets, and ramps. The back box also is used to attract players. The back glass art is crafted to draw players to a certain machine. It is usually done by a professional artist.

The Pinball Playfield

The pinball playfield is usually made of wood with several layers of paint and finish. The playfield is inclined at an angle toward the player, creating a hill on which the ball moves by gravity. The bumpers, ramps, and flippers are all mounted onto the playfield. All these pieces are wired into the main control board in the back glass area so that the computer can tell where the ball is and give points. Once the start button is pressed, a ball from the trough is placed into the **launch lane** in front of the **plunger.** On some machines, you still have to pull the plunger back and let it go to launch the ball into play. On many newer machines, however, there is simply a button to press.

Jackpot!

Scoring in pinball games is not easy for most amateur pinball players. Your score is kept on display, at the base of the back glass. Hitting individual bumpers and targets scores some points.

Replay

Before your last ball, you usually see a screen flash up on the display saying something like "Replay Value." This means that if you reach this point total, you receive a free game.

Tilt!

Another part of pinball is the **tilt sensor.** It makes sure players don't cheat. By shaking the machine, a player is able to influence how the ball travels on the playfield and then may score. Depending on the machine, you might immediately lose your ball, or you might get a warning before all the flippers stop working and your ball goes down the drain.

1.3 Mini-Lesson: Using Non-Fiction Every Day

Non-Fiction
Component: _X_ Genre   ___Structure   ___Style   ___Element

Process: ___Observation   ___Collaboration   _X_ Practice   ___Performance

Set-Up: _X_ Individual   ___Small Group   ___Whole Class

Goal: Students understand that non-fiction has different purposes and intent. They realize that non-fiction is functional.

Materials
Required: Activity Sheet: Using Non-Fiction Every Day

Procedure: Students use this activity sheet to develop an understanding of the ideas. Students often do not realize how much reading of non-fiction they do daily until they take a closer examination of daily routines such as the ones provided on the activity sheet.

Assessment: Teachers assess students' understanding of the concepts with a follow-up classroom discussion. The dialogue students engage in can help teachers assess their knowledge.

Extension
Activity: As a follow-up to this activity sheet, students can create a personal diary sheet for themselves or their family and record the number of times they use non-fiction daily. Students can go on information hunts and locate different sources of non-fiction they have in their household or their neighbourhood. People from different professions can be invited to the classroom to share information about their jobs and discuss how non-fiction reading plays an important part in their daily lives.

Activity Sheet: Using Non-Fiction Every Day

Non-fiction is such a big part of our lives that sometimes we do not realize how often we use it. The following is the diary of Mr. Webber. See if you can figure out how many times he may have used a piece of non-fiction to assist him and think about what type of non-fiction he may have used.

Non-Fiction Source

7:00 AM	Makes waffles for breakfast from a new recipe.	_____
8:00 AM	Checks the bus schedule, catches the bus, reads his newspaper while riding on the bus.	_____
9:00 AM	At work, receives a request form from co-worker for his assistance with a job.	_____
10:00 AM	Has to fix co-worker's computer. Checks the computer manual.	_____
11:00 AM	Answers his business mail.	_____
12:00 PM	Goes out for lunch, orders items from the menu at a new restaurant he has never tried.	_____
1:00 PM	Makes business phone calls. Has to look up the numbers.	_____
4:00 PM	On his way home, picks up some groceries his wife has written on a list for him.	_____
5:00 PM	Checks his email. Gets some information on some coins (his hobby is coin collecting).	_____
5:30 PM	Looks up the value of coins in his book of coins.	_____
7:00 PM	Mr. Webber and his wife decide to go to a movie. They check show times and reviews to help them decide which movie to see.	_____
9:30 PM	Back home, before going to bed, reads his brochure for the holiday he and his wife will be going on next month.	_____

2. MINI-LESSONS TO ACTIVATE *STRUCTURE*

The activating lessons provided here are designed to offer students background information about the structures of non-fiction.

2.1 Mini-Lesson: Introducing Different Structures

Non-Fiction Component:	___Genre	_X_ Structure	___Style	___Element
Process:	_X_ Observation	___Collaboration	___Practice	___Performance
Set-Up:	___Individual	___Small Group	_X_ Whole Class	

Goal: Students are exposed to sources of different structures and provided with a clear definition so that they may be able to identify the structures independently.

Materials Required: Samples of structures sheets

Procedure: Collect samples of structures and save them to file folders for students to access as sources for reading and modelling for writing. Share different structures in a format similar to book talks. Provide students with a definition of the structure and then share examples.

Assessment: Teachers make ongoing classroom observations of students engaging in non-fiction and assess their ability to readily identify different structures. Teachers may choose to do this in the form of mini student conferences.

Extension Activities: Have students independently seek out samples of structures and save them in communal file folders to which other students have access.

SAMPLES OF STRUCTURES

Advertisements

Advertisements are made to try to convince people to look at something, buy something, or do something.

There are two parts to an ad: the words and the picture. The two are put together for an exciting, interesting way of showing something to attract people's attention. The words can be divided into two parts: few words in large print to attract people's attention; and then, in smaller font, a message convincing people about the worth of the product. The picture would then fit with the meaning of the words. Often, the words are made up into a catchy phrase that is easy to remember.

Brochures

A brochure is a type of advertising. It usually comes in the form of a folded piece of paper with written information and pictures. The purpose of a brochure is to convince readers about an idea. There are two main types of brochures: commercial—trying to sell a product or service; and informative—trying to provide information on a topic.

Brochures must catch people's attention and be easy to read so people can get the message quickly. Brochures can include some of the following: diagrams, pictures, maps, special fonts, headlines.

Interviews

An interview can be a written conversation between two people: one person asking questions and the other person providing answers. There are two main purposes of interviews: to learn more information about a person; or to learn more information about a topic from a knowledgeable person.

The writing follows a pattern of question and then answer, each one written in a new section. The question and answer will start with either the letters Q and A or with the names of the people in the interview. Pictures of the interviewer and interviewee may be included.

Postcards

A postcard is a card with space for an address, stamp, and message on one side and a picture that relates information on the other side. They are used for sending messages by mail without an envelope. Postcards relate information between two people. The person sending the postcard is sharing personal experiences or wishes to pass on a message to the reader. Since the space on the card is limited, the message will often be in point form or will try to get the main idea across with the minimum amount of writing. Many postcards illustrate a place (although they can be on any topic). A small amount of information about the illustration may be found on the card.

Recipes

A recipe is a set of instructions that shows how to prepare or make something. The most common recipes demonstrate the preparation of food. Recipes usually contain the name of the product, the ingredients or materials required, and the steps or techniques needed to complete the project. Recipes follow a proper sequence. Recipe steps are usually written in short sentences. They may be numbered or use a symbol (a dash, dot, or star) to show the reader the next step.

Reviews

A review is the writer's opinion of a piece of work. Some common reviews include those of books, movies, video games, music, art, and television. The writer is either recommending, or advising readers to avoid, the reviewed item. The review is written with personal opinions but the reviewer also provides support for their opinion by giving examples from the piece of work. A reviewer will often judge an item based on a scale. They may rate it on a scale of 1 to 10 or use a star system with a value attached to the number of stars awarded to the item.

2.2 Mini-Lesson: Finding the Right Piece of Non-Fiction

Non-Fiction Component: ___Genre X Structure ___Style ___Element

Process: X Observation ___Collaboration ___Practice X Performance

Set-Up: X Individual ___Small Group ___Whole Class

Goal: Students develop an understanding that readers of non-fiction use material to obtain information and they may be able to get it from more than one source (or structure of non-fiction). Depending on the intent, the reader usually wants the most efficient source from which to obtain that information.

Materials Required: Finding the Right Piece of Non-Fiction Worksheet

Procedure: The worksheet encourages students to discuss options for seeking information. For students to be effective readers of non-fiction, they must understand how non-fiction can be functional, and can provide answers. The activity sheet reinforces the concept that more than one non-fiction structure can be used to achieve their goals. It is useful to display a list of structures in the room for students to refer to while they complete their sheet. Small groups can discuss their possible choices of non-fiction.

Assessment: Teachers assess students' ability to use appropriate sources. Some students may find answers to the questions, but not from the most efficient source. For example, finding the population of China in a book about the country may be correct, but not as efficient as using an almanac with world populations. In these cases, often the student is unfamiliar with the structure. The teacher may have a small-group meeting with these students to introduce the non-fiction source.

Extension Activities: This activity is known as Information Scavenger Hunt. Students will need a series of periods in the school library to do this activity. A set of questions is written on index cards. Students first use library resources to find an answer to a question. Then, they orally tell the teacher the answer and have the source on hand for verification. The goal for students is to answer as many questions as possible, accurately and with speed. Therefore, being able to locate source material is an important part of the task.

Finding the Right Piece of Non-Fiction Worksheet

Non-fiction can provide us with answers to many questions. We have several choices of structures of non-fiction to help us find our answers. Which structure of non-fiction would be the best for each situation listed below?

Nancy wants to visit her aunt across the city and isn't sure how to find her street. Which structure of non-fiction can help her? _____

Ron wants to buy a new computer, but isn't sure which is the best type to get. Which structure of non-fiction can help him? _____

Chris wants to make a great dinner for his family, but is not sure what to cook. Which structure of non-fiction can help him? _____

Jenny has a leak in her sink and needs a plumber, but does not know one. Which structure of non-fiction can help her find one? _____

Larry wants to learn how to play chess, but does not know the rules. Which structure of non-fiction can help him learn the rules? _____

Jasmine wants to know what the word "radical" means. Which structure of non-fiction can tell her the meaning of the word? _____

Dan is doing a project on India and needs to know the capital city of the country. Which structure of non-fiction can help him? _____

Wendy is planning a holiday this winter, but is not sure where she wants to go. Which structure of non-fiction can help her? _____

INFORMATION SCAVENGER HUNT

The following sample questions for a scavenger hunt can be written on index cards and researched by students in a school library.

Who invented the airplane?

What year was Martin Luther King born?

Who painted the *Mona Lisa*?

Where was Wayne Gretzky born?

Who wrote the book, *Ella Enchanted?*

What is the capital city of Australia?

What colours are on Italy's flag?

In what country is Mount Everest?

What is the population of Alaska?

How many different definitions are there for the word "panel"?

What is a yucca?

How many keys are on a piano?

What is a typhoon?

What colour is a hyena?

How many rings are on the Olympic symbol?

How tall is the Empire State Building?

What year was the book, *The Cat in the Hat,* first published?

How many provinces does Canada have?

In what state is the Grand Canyon located?

Which is the largest planet in the solar system?

How heavy can a beluga whale be?

Name a country that is a neighbour to France.

What does the word *marsupial* mean?

How many pieces are on a chessboard?

Name a poem written by Shel Silverstein.

When was the zipper invented?

Who was Amelia Earhart?

When did the *Titanic* sink?

When was the television invented?

How big is the country of Switzerland?

Name an ingredient used in lasagna.

3. MINI-LESSONS TO ACTIVATE *STYLE*

These forms of style used by authors of non-fiction are directly related to the reading strategies used by non-fiction readers. The following mini-lessons activate an awareness of the connection between the reading and writing process.

3.1 Mini-Lesson: Using Background Information

Non-Fiction Component:	___Genre	___Structure	X Style	___Element
Process:	___Observation	___Collaboration	X Practice	___Performance
Set-Up:	X Individual	___Small Group	___Whole Class	

Goal: Students learn that "background information" refers to all the ideas we have stored in our mind from our prior learning. Background information can help us figure out what an author is trying to say. All that we learn and discover becomes our background information.

Materials Required: Activity Sheet: Using Background Information

Procedure: Students' independent work with the activity sheet is followed up with class discussion.

Assessment: In small-group guided reading sessions, teachers observe students' ability to apply technique and strategy.

Extension Activities: Have students reflect in their Reading Record on their ability to use techniques and strategies in their independent reading. Pose a question to students, such as: When has your background information helped you in reading? Follow up with Using Background Information Worksheet II.

Activity Sheet: Using Background Information

What we already know, our "background information," is important because it can help us in our reading. We use these ideas to help us figure out what a writer intends. Using background information can help us form a clearer picture in our minds of what the author is trying to say.

Read each of the sentences and answer the questions. As you are working, think about the specific background information you have that helps you to answer each question.

Billy zoomed out at 3:30 and headed onto the big yellow vehicle.

What is Billy doing? _____

How do you know this? _____

Carrie had to finish her homework. She slipped her diskette in the drive and opened up her story on the screen. All she had to do was edit, then print it out.

How is Carrie doing her homework? _____

How do you know this? _____

Harry stood at the plate. He was ready to hit a homer, not bunt it as the coach said. Besides, Harry knew the pitches would be fastballs, and he was good at hitting those.

What is Harry doing? _____

How do you know this? _____

Teal and Lauren sat in the big room filled with chairs. At the emergency desk, people stood waiting. All around the halls, people wearing white were moving wheelchairs and stretchers.

Where are Teal and Lauren? _____

How do you know this? _____

Cole placed his tackle box on the ground. He opened it up and searched for the hook and bait he was going to use. Then, he checked his line on the reel. He was almost set.

What is Cole doing? _____

How do you know this? _____

Ellen looked in the store mirror. She liked the colour of the clothing but the zipper did not go up and down easily. Besides, there was no hood, and she would need one in January. Mind you, it was long enough to cover most of her body, plus it had a really nice fur trim on it.

What is Ellen trying on? _____

How do you know this? _____

_____

Next time you are reading, think about how many times you use background information to figure out things the author does not mention. You'll be surprised at how often you use it.

Using Background Information Worksheet II

Name: _____   Date: _____

You have learned that what we already know helps us to understand what happens in stories that we read. What you are using is called *background information*. It helps you make sense of new ideas. Read the following short paragraphs. By using background information, answer each of the questions.

Sally had the dough rolled into the pan. She spread on the tomato sauce, sprinkled pepperoni on, and topped it with shredded cheese. Then, she placed the pan in the oven to cook her lunch.

What is Sally's lunch? _____

How do you know this? _____

Mel noticed one of the tires was flat. A pedal was loose and the chain had to be repaired. The brakes were okay, but the handlebars had to be tightened.

What is Mel fixing? _____

How do you know this? _____

Kathy studied each animal at the zoo. She stood in front of the cage and watched an animal come out swinging. The animal used its tail to swing from branch to branch, then dropped down and started eating a banana.

What kind of animal is Kathy watching? _____

How do you know this? _____

Franny watched the television. The countdown began. As the count of one came on, the screen was filled with a large explosive sound, and flames shot out of the engines as the vehicle started moving straight up into the sky.

What is Franny watching? _____

How do you know this? _____

Margaret listened to the report on the radio. The winds were getting stronger. A large, swirling cloud had been spotted in the sky. It had already sucked up cars and the force of the winds had destroyed homes.

What kind of weather is approaching? _____

How do you know this? _____

Callie moved across the field. She stopped and chewed on some fine fresh grass. She neighed as her owner came towards her with the lasso rope. Callie galloped the other way and jumped the fence.

Who is Callie? _____

How do you know this? _____

Frank phoned Tom to make arrangements for their trip they had planned for the weekend. After talking to Tom, Frank asked him if he could hand the phone over to Mom.

What is Frank and Tom's relationship? _____

How do you know this? _____

Donald did up his laces. His blades were nice and sharp. He put on his helmet, and grabbed his gloves and stick. He was ready. He could barely wait to get out there and start taking shots at the net.

What is Donald going to do? _____

How do you know this? _____

3.2 Mini-Lesson: Using Inferences

Non-Fiction
Component: ___Genre   ___Structure   _X_ Style   ___Element

Process: ___Observation   ___Collaboration   _X_ Practice   ___Performance

Set-Up: _X_ Individual   ___Small Group   ___Whole Class

Goal: Students develop an understanding of the process of inferring and the ability to "read between the lines" to extract important pieces of information.

Materials Required: Activity Sheet: Using Inferences

Procedure: Students first do independent work with the worksheet, followed by class discussion. With this lesson, teachers begin to look at specific skills in the process of reading non-fiction. The lesson is a good follow-up to the one on background information. While the previous lesson shows students how important background knowledge is to reading, here they learn how to apply their knowledge to a specific skill: inferring.

Assessment: In small-group guided reading sessions, teachers note students' ability to apply technique and strategy.

Extension Activities: Have students reflect in their Reading Record on their ability to use techniques and strategies in their independent reading. Have students write about a reading experience in which they had to infer meaning.

Follow up with Using Inferences Worksheet II.

Activity Sheet: Using Inferences

Sometimes when we are reading, not all the information is written down. Sometimes we have to "read between the lines." What we are doing is figuring out an invisible message. This invisible message is called an *inference*. When we try to figure out these messages, it is called *inferring*.

Can you read between the lines to figure out what the "invisible message" is?

When Amber came home, her mother was standing at the front door with her arms crossed, and tapping her foot.

What message can you figure out about Amber's mom? _____

Sweat was dripping off Ron's face, his body tingled all over, and his heart was pounding, but still Ron went up on the stage.

What message can you figure out about Ron? _____

Jane sighed. At the birthday party she had to sit next to the boy who bothered her, and then they served strawberry ice cream. Jane was allergic to strawberries.

What message can you figure out about Jane? _____

When Harry and Sara got home, all the furniture was thrown around the room. Then they noticed the kitchen window had been smashed.

What message can you figure out about Harry and Sara's house? _____

John took a big mouthful of the food from his plate. He frowned, gulped it down, and took a sip of water to wash away the taste.

What message can you figure out about John and his food? _____

Carl huffed and puffed as he carried the box inside. His arms started to hurt, and he could feel the box starting to slip out of his hands.

What message can you figure out about Carl's box? _____

Using Inferences Worksheet II

What message is hidden inside the following paragraphs?

James could not stop thinking about tomorrow. Maybe he would forget how to hit the baseball. Maybe the other kids would laugh at him if he couldn't catch the ball. Oh, why did he sign up for the team in the first place?

What message can you figure out about James? _____

Lindy could not put the book down. In fact, she was so into her book that she did not even hear when the visitors rang the doorbell.

What message can you figure out about Lindy's book? _____

George was going crazy. He thought he had left his keys on the table. George started throwing papers off the table in his search.

What message can you figure out about George's keys? _____

That was it! First, Ted's brother took his jacket without asking him and now he had found him going into his desk drawer without asking.

What message can you figure out about Ted? _____

It was not an ordinary day. People were late for work because cars would not start. Children were not allowed outside for recess. The few people who were outside wore extra clothing.

What message can you figure out about the day? _____

Jenny could hardly move. It was even hard to sit down. Her skin was deep red all over. She knew she should not have stayed outside so long.

What message can you figure out about Jenny? _____

3.3 Mini-Lesson: Learning New Vocabulary

**Non-Fiction
Component:**   ___Genre   ___Structure   X Style   ___Element

Process: ___Observation   ___Collaboration X Practice   ___Performance

Set-Up: X Individual   ___Small Group   ___Whole Class

Goal: Students are exposed to skills to help them understand new vocabulary. One effective strategy is using the surrounding text to help identify the meaning of a new word.

**Materials
Required:**   Activity Sheet: Figuring out Mystery Words

Procedure: Non-fiction reading is one of the genres in which students are most likely to encounter unfamiliar vocabulary, which often can be technical in nature and difficult to pronounce. Students need new skills to help them understand new vocabulary. Although teachers should promote the use of dictionaries, they also want students to expand their repertoire. This activity is one strategy that helps students do that. Students enjoy this activity of taking nonsense words and figuring out their meaning, using surrounding print. Once again, this activity always leaves some students amazed at how much they already know about the reading process.

Assessment: In small-group guided reading sessions, teachers note students' ability to apply technique and strategy.

**Extension
Activities:** Have students reflect in their Reading Record on their ability to use techniques and strategies in their independent reading. Students write about new vocabulary they learn and how they were able to discover the meaning. Follow up with Activity Sheet II: Figuring out Mystery Words.

Activity Sheet: Figuring out Mystery Words

Sometimes you are reading and everything is going along well until you come to a word that you don't know. What do you do? First, you should try to sound it out, break it down into parts, and see if you can say the word and recognize it.

Other times, you may be able to pronounce the word, but still do not know what it means. You could look the word up in a dictionary. This is wise to do, but sometimes you do not want to stop your reading and lose your thoughts. There is another way to figure out the meaning of a word without going to the dictionary. Often, readers can use the words that surround a mystery word to figure out the meaning. While this may not give you the exact dictionary meaning, you can learn enough about the word to understand what is going on without disturbing your reading.

After you are finished reading, you can look the word up in the dictionary. You may be surprised at how close you were to understanding the meaning, just by using your skills and the surrounding print.

Read each short paragraph. Use clues in the story to help you figure out what each mystery word means.

Tomorrow, Ronald is going on a loopera. Ronald hasn't been on a loopera in a whole year. Last year, when he was on a loopera, he went to Disneyland. This year, Ronald's loopera will be one week in Mexico. Ronald likes to go to warm places when he takes his loopera in the winter.

What is a loopera? _____

Annabelle is so proud of her tweezle. Her brother got a tweezle last year, but his was for chess. Annabelle's tweezle was for swimming. Annabelle decided to keep her tweezle on a shelf so others could see it. After all, not everyone gets a tweezle for coming in first in the city's Swim Competition.

What is a tweezle? _____

John is a very deppy person. People like being around John because he is so deppy. John will play all kinds of tricks on people and tell real deppy jokes to make people laugh.

What is deppy? _____

Activity Sheet II: Figuring out Mystery Words

Use the words around each mystery word to figure out its meaning.

The freeglefriemer would soon be here. Joanne could hardly wait for the freeglefriemer. Joanne was going to ski, skate, and watch movies on the freeglefriemer. Today was Wednesday, two more days till the freeglefriemer.

What is a freeglefriemer? _____

Susan shnarps every Friday evening at a class. She also practises shnarping whenever she has a spare moment. Most of the time, Susan gets her brother to be her partner for shnarping. Susan thinks that really fast music is the best for shnarping.

What is shnarping? _____

Cal is a very parfloopy person. His mom always tells him he is parfloopy every time she sees his room. Most of the time his room is so parfloopy that there is no room to walk on the floor. Even at school, Cal is parfloopy. He can never find anything in his desk.

What is parfloopy? _____

Teal and Cole both had new spoofettes. Teal's spoofette was green and Cole's was red. Teal's spoofette was much warmer than Cole's because it had a hood. Cole also had trouble with the zipper on his spoofette.

What is a spoofette? _____

Mary's joony was the cutest in the whole neighbourhood. Every time she would walk down the street with her joony, people would stop and ask to see it. Mary could also get her joony to do tricks. Every time her joony did a trick, she would give it a bone.

What is a joony? _____

Jodie loved going to the bricbat as much as she could. The bricbat that was down her street was her favourite. Every time Jodie got her allowance, she would head to the bricbat. She would buy all kinds of candy at the bricbat.

What is a bricbat? _____

3.4 Mini-Lesson: Remembering Important Details— Main Idea and Supporting Details

Non-Fiction
Component: ___Genre ___Structure X Style ___Element

Process: ___Observation ___Collaboration X Practice ___Performance

Set-Up: X Individual ___Small Group ___Whole Class

Goal: Students learn how to sift through relevant and irrelevant facts that pertain to the main idea of a reading passage. In many situations when readers are having difficulty with non-fiction, it is because they are finding it difficult to sort out relevant details from irrelevant bits of information. Non-fiction can be filled with many pieces of trivia that may be interesting but are an aside to the main concept. Often, readers who are having difficulty are trying to remember every small detail or fact and the main idea becomes muddled up with other facts.

Materials
Required: Activity Sheet: Remembering Important Details

Procedure: Students receive short paragraphs to read and highlight the important facts. Students must be able to identify details that are not relevant, and to rationalize why a fact is not pertinent to the main idea of the piece. As the students become experienced with determining the relevance of information, they will be able to apply the skills to their personal reading.

Assessment: In small-group guided reading sessions, teachers note students' ability to apply technique and strategy.

Extension
Activities: Have students reflect in their Reading Record on their ability to use techniques and strategies in their independent reading by doing retellings.

Activity Sheet: Remembering Important Details

All that we read is important. The information an author has put into a piece of writing is there for a reason: it may be there to give us a clear picture in our minds, to make us curious, to give us information, or to amuse us. Even though all information is important, this does not mean we have to remember every detail. This is especially true as we begin to read longer pieces. Not all information can be remembered. It means that, as we read, we have to make decisions about which facts are important just for the moment, and which ones are important to keep in our minds.

Read the following parts of a story. Decide which facts are important for only the moment, and which facts you may need to remember for later.

Example:

The woman pushed open the big oak doors with the large, golden doorknobs, with such force that they slammed against the back of the wall. She walked across the crowded dance floor, up to the tables. She stared down at the man sitting there and then violently slapped him in the face. She then turned and walked back out those doors.

What details are not important enough to remember for the future?
Probably, the type of door and the doorknobs are not important to remember.

What is important to remember?
Probably, it is important to remember that she entered a dance floor and slapped a man in the face.

Read each of the short paragraphs. Decide which information is relevant and which facts are not.

George sat down on his green, soft, comfy couch, which was filled with pillows. He turned on the television and started flipping through the channels. There didn't seem to be anything on that he wanted to watch. Then, one channel caught his attention. A tornado warning had just been issued. George looked out the window and noticed the trees were blowing and bending.

Which facts are not important to remember? _____

What is important to remember? _____

Martha stepped into the kitchen, very excited. She wanted to make a fabulous dinner for her friend Jane, who was coming to visit. Martha had not seen Jane in five years. It would be so nice to see her again. Martha pulled out the tomatoes, peppers, noodles, eggs, milk, and lettuce, and placed the food on the counter.

Which facts are not important to remember? _____

What is important to remember? _____

Gerry sat down at his pulsar super-turbo XJ-2 computer and began to type. He was nervous. He had to get his assignment done today and it had to be at least ten pages long. Gerry had not even started yet. He had a lot of work ahead of him and it was already 10:00 PM.

Which facts are not important to remember? _____

What is important to remember? _____

3.5 Mini-Lesson: Drawing Conclusions

Non-Fiction
Component: ___Genre   ___Structure   _X_ Style   ___Element

Process: ___Observation   ___Collaboration   _X_ Practice   ___Performance

Set-Up: _X_ Individual   ___Small Group   _X_ Whole Class

Goal: Students develop effective strategies for making predictions. To be able to do this, a reader must have experience in drawing conclusions, based on the facts. Drawing conclusions is very similar to a reader's ability to draw inferences from data. The difference is that when readers synthesize or draw conclusions, they collect many bits of information to form a larger idea. When they come to some conclusions, they can use this information as background knowledge to form more accurate predictions.

Materials Required: Activity Sheet: Drawing Conclusions from What You Read

Procedure: Students read a short paragraph and then articulate a conclusion, based on what they have read. As they draw conclusions about the paragraphs, the teacher leads a discussion of what might happen next, based on what they think has already occurred. In the small-group reading instruction, the teacher will have students regularly drawing conclusions about the material they read.

Assessment: In small-group guided reading sessions, teachers note students' ability to apply technique and strategy.

Extension Activities: Have students reflect in their Reading Record on their ability to use techniques and strategies in their independent reading. Students write a summary about their reading.

Activity Sheet: Drawing Conclusions from What You Read

Readers get many ideas from print, and they use these ideas to draw a conclusion. A conclusion is a "big" idea that can be formed from little bits of information that are "proof" for the big idea. Why is it important to develop conclusions? Once you have determined the big ideas, they can help you predict future items found in the writing. Look at the following example to help you get a better understanding of how to draw conclusions and why this is so important.

Billy walked into the classroom and pushed past the other students, as he did every morning. He took the pencil off the desk of the girl who sat in front of him and stuck it in his pocket. No one ever looked at Billy because they knew they would get an ugly glare from him.

What conclusions can you form about Billy? (He's a really nasty sort of person.) Why is this important to know?

The next section begins with a new student's moving into the classroom and being assigned the seat next to Billy. Based on the conclusions drawn about Billy's character, can you predict how Billy may start to treat the new student?

If you said Billy's treatment of the new student would be terrible, you're probably correct. You made an accurate prediction, based on earlier conclusions.

Read the following short paragraphs and form some conclusions, based on what you read.

Tammy was going for a visit to her cousin Mary's house for the first time. When Tammy's family pulled up in front of the house, she was surprised at what she saw. The front gate was broken, and paint was peeling off the house. Inside, there was not enough furniture for everybody to have a seat. Mary was wearing the same clothes as the last time Tammy saw her, except there were more holes in them. When Tammy went to the kitchen to get a drink of water, she noticed most of the cupboards were bare.

What conclusions can you draw? _____

_____

_____

Mac and Josh returned to their campsite to find it a complete wreck. All the packs of food had been ripped open, but the items in jars had not been opened. Their tent was shredded in pieces, as if something had been scratched down its side. The two boys followed some prints leading to the forest but quickly stopped as they heard a growling sound ahead of them.

What conclusions can you draw? _____

_____

_____

Benny had enough today! He was going home. He ran out of tissue and he was still sniffling. Not only that, his head felt as if someone was banging away at it. All day at school, he had felt strange. One minute he was chilly, needing a sweater, and right after, he was sweating. Now, to make matters worse, he was getting pains in his stomach.

What conclusions can you draw? _____

_____

_____

Jane and Emma went bike riding to the park. On the way there, they saw a small, young boy sitting on the curb by himself. An hour later on their way back home, they saw the same boy walking back and forth on the sidewalk. He looked as if he had been crying. It was starting to get dark out and it seemed as if no one was around looking for the wee lad.

What conclusions can you draw? _____

_____

_____.

3.6 Mini-Lesson: Distinguishing Fact from Opinion

Non-Fiction Component: ___Genre ___Structure _X_ Style ___Element

Process: ___Observation ___Collaboration _X_ Practice ___Performance

Set-Up: _X_ Individual ___Small Group ___Whole Class

Goal: Students develop a complete understanding of the differences between fact and opinion. This is a crucial skill for a critical reader. Students often mistake opinion for being only false information, and all fact as truth. Teachers should emphasize that fact and opinion are not as simply defined as these singular concepts.

Materials Required: Activity Sheet: Fact and Opinion

Procedure: This activity is designed to help students distinguish between fact and opinion but also to help them realize that opinion is not necessarily false, but a point of view that must be closely examined by the reader. This lesson works well when teachers want to introduce blended texts or Info fiction.

Assessment: In small-group guided reading sessions, teachers note students' ability to apply technique and strategy.

Extension Activities: Have students reflect in their Reading Record on their ability to use techniques and strategies in their independent reading. Students write their opinions on a topic they have read. Follow up with Fact and Opinion Worksheet II.

Activity Sheet: Fact and Opinion

Throughout your life, you will read a great deal of information. Some of it will be fact and some will be opinion. What is the difference? A *fact* is something that is true about a subject and can be tested or proven. A fact does not change from person to person, or from place to place. Facts are things that we know have happened.

An *opinion* is what someone thinks about that subject. Opinions are often beliefs. The author believes it may have happened or believes it may be true but does not have the complete proof.

Sometimes it can be hard to tell whether a statement is a fact or an opinion. Read each of the statements and decide if they are fact or opinion. Write **F** for fact and **O** for opinion.

1. Sunsets are beautiful to look at. _____

2. Oranges are a source of vitamins for your body. _____

3. More people own blue cars than pink cars. _____

4. People over 30 years are considered old. _____

5. Oranges taste better than apples. _____

6. The sun sets in the west. _____

7. In many countries, you must be 18 years old to be an adult. _____

8. People with red cars drive faster than people with blue cars. _____

9. The earth is the most beautiful planet in our solar system. _____

10. The sun is classified as a star. _____

11. Boys are taller than girls. _____

12. Girls are smarter than boys. _____

13. There are more right-handed people than left-handed people. _____

14. Coin collecting is fun. _____

15. Many newspapers are published daily. _____

16. All newspapers are published daily. _____

17. Wednesday is the fourth day of the week. _____

Fact and Opinion Worksheet II

Read the paragraph below. After reading it, decide which information in it can be classified as fact and which information can be classified as opinion.

At the Midville Community gym yesterday, Albertson School's female volleyball team defeated Ashton School by a score of 42 to 30. It was a fantastic game, with Albertson school being the dominant team throughout the game. The Ashton players were great sports. Their coach, Mrs. Virginia Bertrand, said, "We really needed to win tonight to get a place in the finals." But Albertson was too good, particularly around the net. Carol Dupont of Ashton sprained her ankle diving for the ball and had to leave the game halfway. Brenda Wiebe of Albertson was superb in her serving. Next week Albertson plays Wender School, a game they should easily win.

Fact

_____

_____

_____

_____

_____

_____

_____

_____

_____

Opinion

_____

_____

_____

_____

_____

_____

_____

_____

_____

4. MINI-LESSONS TO ACTIVATE *ELEMENTS*

The activating lessons provided here are designed to offer students background information about certain elements/features and then allow them to follow up with an examination of actual text found within the classroom. Similar informational sheets can be designed for other features.

4.1 Mini-Lesson: The Importance of Graphs

Non-Fiction Component: ___Genre   ___Structure   ___Style   <u>X</u> Element

Process: <u>X</u> Observation   ___Collaboration   ___Practice   ___Performance

Set-Up: ___Individual   ___Small Group   <u>X</u> Whole Class

Goal: Students learn to use graphs as an aid to gain further knowledge on a specific topic.

Materials Required: Information Sheet: The Importance of Graphs

Procedure: The information sheet is a starting point for a class discussion on the relevance of graphs in non-fiction reading material. Students often believe features such as graphs only retell existing print information. The teacher should point out to students that graphs often can explain important data in efficient formats.

Assessment: In small-group guided reading sessions, teachers note students' ability to use the feature.

Extension Activities: The Information Sheet provided integrates well with math lessons. After reading it, students can refer to graphs in math texts. This creates a useful reminder to students that textbook material such as a math book is a form of non-fiction. Students can follow up this lesson by creating their own graphs and seeking out other forms of text that use graphs.

THE IMPORTANCE OF GRAPHS

Graphs are used for many reasons, and found in many places. People use them to notice changes, to compare items, and to learn new information. We find them in newspapers, magazines, and books. There are several different types of graphs, but two of the most common types are line and bar graphs. To begin to analyze graphs, read the following information.

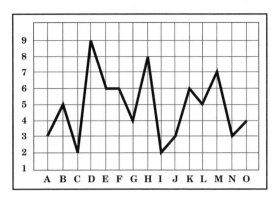

Line Graph: Frequency of Letters

- The first thing to notice is the title of the graph. The title should give you some explanation about the topic of the graph.

- Graphs have starting lines known as *axes*. There is a horizontal and a vertical axis. Each axis is like a ruler, ready to measure something. Check out each axis.

- The vertical axis measures how much, how many, or how often. The horizontal axis shows the type of information being studied. Both axes should have labels that help you figure out what is being measured.

- Reading each axis and the information plotted on them will help you gain new knowledge.

- The line graph shows patterns and changes in the information, and a bar graph compares the information.

See if you can locate graphs in a piece of non-fiction. Study them. Do they give you any information? Try to locate some other types of graphs. Notice how they are similar to, or different from, the line and bar graphs.

4.2 Mini-Lesson: Table of Contents

Non-Fiction Component:	___Genre	___Structure	___Style	X Element
Process:	X Observation	___Collaboration	___Practice	___Performance
Set-Up:	___Individual	___Small Group	X Whole Class	

Goal: Students learn the value of a table of contents feature and how it can be used to locate information in an efficient manner.

Materials Required: Sample Information Sheet: *Learning All About Italy* Table of Contents; Activity Sheet: Examining the Table of Contents

Procedure: The sample sheet and questions activate an examination of the table of contents. Many students will briefly skim a contents page, while others completely ignore it. Showing students the advantages to analyzing the contents page will help them to do further research.

Assessment: In small-group guided reading sessions, teachers note students' ability to use the feature.

Extension Activities: This activity can be recreated with any existing text in the classroom related to different curricula.

SAMPLE INFORMATION SHEET: *Learning All About Italy*

Table of Contents

Activity Sheet: Examining the Table of Contents

The table of contents is the first page you should turn to when you are reading a book. The table of contents can be an important tool for you. It can tell you if a book has the information you are seeking, how much information it has, and how to find it quickly.

The table of contents is a directory. It can lead you to certain pages with specific pieces of information. Some tables of contents will have subheadings that group information under one main topic. Look at the table of contents page provided to you. Use it to help you answer the following questions.

1. What page would you turn to if you wanted to know the capital city of Italy? ____

2. Which section looks as if it may have the most information on a subject? _____

3. You want to know how long Italy has been a country. To which section or page would you turn? _____

4. You are seeking information on national holidays in Italy. Where would you turn to see if the information is in the book? _____

5. The Leaning Tower of Pisa is a place many tourists visit. On which page could you possibly locate information about it? _____

4.3 Mini-Lesson: Finding Elements in Non-Fiction

**Non-Fiction
Component:**   ___Genre   ___Structure   ___Style   X Element

Process: ___Observation   ___Collaboration   ___Practice   X Performance

Set-Up: X Individual   ___Small Group   ___Whole Class

Goal: As students pay closer attention to identifiable features in
                 a piece of non-fiction, they start to use them independently,
                 developing a stronger comprehension of the material.

**Materials
Required:**   File Card: Finding Elements in Non-Fiction

Procedure: After students have read a piece of non-fiction, they fill out a
                 features index card, indicating the specific elements/features
                 they have located and used during their reading. This exercise
                 provides them with time to reflect on the processes they have
                 used. Students collaborate by sharing their file cards with others
                 and attaching the card to the piece of writing for other students
                 to use in the future. Once students have been introduced to this
                 activity, it can become a part of a reading routine.

Assessment: Teachers review the file cards filled in by students, noting their
                 ability to identify features independently.

**Extension
Activities:**   Have students reflect in their Reading Record on their ability
                 to identify and use the features in their independent reading.

File Card: Finding Elements in Non-Fiction

Title of Non-Fiction: _____

Book: ☐   Article: ☐

Main Topic: _____

Check all the elements you find in the piece:

☐ bold print   ☐ charts   ☐ captions   ☐ diagrams
☐ flow charts   ☐ fonts   ☐ footnotes   ☐ graphs
☐ glossaries   ☐ guide words   ☐ headings/subheadings
☐ indexes   ☐ italicized words   ☐ labels   ☐ maps
☐ pictures   ☐ pronunciation guides   ☐ sidebars
☐ timelines   ☐ tables of contents

Which element did you find the most helpful to you? _____

How did it help you? _____

PLANNING FURTHER LESSONS

There are many potential mini-lessons that can be generated for non-fiction material. In order to meet the varied needs of students as they engage in non-fiction reading, the teacher must regularly look for examples, highlight information for students, and discuss processes with them.

The teacher continually revises, reworks, and introduces information to fit the needs of the students. A system of organization can assist the teacher for this work. It is helpful to have a structure at hand to be used for lesson planning. On the next two pages is the template that has been used for the mini-lessons contained in this resource book. It may prove to be helpful for teachers when planning their own resource material. The template can be modified to suit specific needs or used in a fashion similar to that found within these pages. The lesson planner template can also assist with manageable record keeping. The template becomes a source for quick referral when working with small groups on the guided reading process.

Lesson Planner Template

Non-Fiction Feature: ___Genre   ___Structure

                           ___Style   ___Element

Process: ___Observation   ___Collaboration

                           ___Practice   ___Performance

Set-Up: ___Individual   ___Small Group   ___Whole Class

Goals for Students: _____

_____

_____

_____

Materials Required: _____

_____

_____

Procedure: _____

_____

_____

Assessment: _____

_____

_____

Extension Activities: _____

_____

_____

Further Notes: _____

_____

_____

CHAPTER FOUR

SUCCESSFUL SMALL-GROUP INSTRUCTION

Reading non-fiction is part of the entire learning process. It is not relegated to one specific curriculum or one specific methodology. Non-fiction material is used in whole-class settings, by individuals, and in small-group instruction for many different reasons. For example, students may engage in non-fiction as part of independent reading. Non-fiction may be a part of a whole-group instruction related to the writing process. Students may engage in non-fiction material to research in areas of social studies or science. The opportunities for engaging in non-fiction text are limitless.

Small-group instruction has always been an effective method for teaching, especially when we are engaging students in new topics of information or demonstrating new skills. Since many of the components of non-fiction are new to students, the small-group setting is an ideal practice for student learning. There are many values to small-group instruction, including the following:

- The teacher has the ability to create positive working relationships with students and to get to know students.
- Small-group instruction allows students to explore more material at a greater depth.
- The opportunity in a small group to adjust the material to fit individual needs means the learning process becomes more meaningful for students.
- Students who feel reluctant to participate in large-group situations are willing to take more risks in the small-group setting and, therefore, engage more with the material.

In 1998, the Columbus Ohio National Middle School Association published its report, *This We Believe: Developmentally Responsive Middle Level Schools*. Its extensive research confirmed there are many advantages for students to work in small-group settings.

- In general, students prefer active learning activities such as interaction with peers in learning situations. The interactive small-group setting provides greater motivation.
- Each student has their own developmental level, due to factors such as socio-economic and cultural background, and prior experiences. Each student requires individualized educational plans. Small-group work can address these individual needs.
- Collaboration and cooperation increase achievement. Different forms of group work should be used, depending on the purpose, with students grouped by interest, or by common need.

Further testament comes from educational experts such as Nancy Atwell, who states in her book, *In the Middle: Writing, Reading, and Learning with Adolescents,* "Learning is more likely to happen when they are not engaged alone, but are grouped so that as they engage together, they may learn from each other." (p. 38)

The value of small-group instruction is acknowledged, but much discussion still centres on the purpose and procedures of the methodology. Many dynamics occur when small-group instruction takes place. The teacher must consider many factors when planning small-group instruction: the appropriate number of students in a group; the makeup of the group (including personalities and needs); and the logistics of running the group (including time, space, and materials).

Looking at some of the fundamentals of small-group instruction provides the teacher with an opportunity to analyze, evaluate, and implement practices that are most beneficial to students. Some may wonder about the need for examining small-group instruction when the focus is on non-fiction, but this examination is important because it helps to create a foundation. Small-group instruction has many variables for successful implementation. If these principles are examined carefully, then there is less chance they will have to be addressed when the teacher and students are engaged in learning non-fiction components.

THE NATURE OF SMALL-GROUP INSTRUCTION

The following questions are useful to consider when planning small-group instruction for non-fiction studies.

What is the purpose for working with students in a small group?
The purpose enables focus on the goals and objectives for the students.

What is it we want the students to gain from the experience?
The teacher must personally answer this question before proceeding.

What form should the small group take on to achieve this goal?
Physical considerations must be accounted for in order for students to achieve the goals and gain from the experience. How many students should be in the small group? Are there enough materials? What physical space is available for the small group?

Setting the Tone for Small-Group Instruction—Behaviours

Management is the key to any successful program run in the classroom. The teacher is managing time, resources, and individuals. If a teacher has an arrangement to work with a small group outside the regular classroom setting, then some management issues, such as space and noise level, are immediately solved. However, for most teachers, small-group instruction takes place in the regular classroom setting.

Teachers want all students to have quality learning time, so the students must be engaged in meaningful activities. However, the teacher requires independence and appropriate behaviours from the students to allow for the opportunity to work with small groups. Some initial prep work is required to teach the whole class appropriate behaviours during small-group instruction time.

Right Tone and Intent for Small-Group Instruction

The classroom can be a place for many different learning styles. At times it is a buzz of activity with high energy, and at other times, the learning environment is a hushed place with a focus on independence rather than on cooperative tasks. The teacher is responsible for providing all kinds of learning environments because not all students work best in the same environment. For small-group instruction, the most effective tone is achieved by having the remaining students work independently. A hushed tone to the room allows the teacher the opportunity to focus attention on the students in the small group.

Helpful Tip: Begin the school year by introducing routines and behaviours that will help students build to the independence required for small-group instruction.

Classroom Voice: Not all students can interpret different tones of voice for different situations. It is important to teach this skill early on in the school year.

Students quickly realize that their voice tone is an important part of communication. Not only do the informal lessons help the large classroom setting, but they are also beneficial for the small-group sessions. Students come into the small group realizing the importance of voice when they begin to communicate with peers.

Helpful Tip: Construct a poster of "Voices in Our Room" at the beginning of the school year. Over the first few weeks, highlight this poster by talking about appropriate voices and the volume required for an activity. Model different voice tones for different situations.

Decision-Making Skills: Decision-making skills are an important part of critical thinking and learning behaviours. One of the most common disruptions for a teacher working with a small group are the questions students have about managing their schoolwork. "I'm done, what do I do now?" is a question that shows the student's inability to apply decision-making skills. This is not a reflection of a student's intelligence, but, rather, inexperience with work habits. Teachers want students to take on responsibility for their learning by knowing what their options are when an assigned piece of work is completed.

Helpful Tip: In the first few weeks of school, show students options for other activities once they have completed their assigned work. You may have to continue to do this throughout the year. However, as time passes, students will need fewer reminders as they take ownership for their learning.

Graphic Organizers: One of the most helpful techniques for students is a graphic organizer. Adults are constantly using daybook planners and to-do lists. Agenda books or lists assist students to decide what to do next. Visual cues placed in the classroom act as reminders and referrals to students and allow the teacher time to focus on the small-group instruction. See the following pages for samples of visual cues to help students monitor their independent work habits.

Helpful Graphic Organizers

Agenda Books   To-Do Lists   Calendar Planners
Class Memo Boards   Class Reminder Charts   Visual Cue Posters

---

The work behaviours mentioned in this section are as important for the success of small-group instruction as the actual group dynamics. Through continued repetition, reinforcement, and modelling, students learn how to create a learning environment that allows teachers the opportunity to work with individuals.

Voices in Our Classroom

Voice Level	Situation
4	A loud voice heard from a distance outside; recess time
3	Loud and clear for an entire audience presentations; speaking to the whole class
2	A hushed, quiet voice, heard by only the people right around you small-group times
1	A soft whisper heard by one other person conferencing; asking for help
0	Very little talking at all working on your own; independent time

Voices in Our Classroom

To-Do List

Name: _____

Date(s): _____

Check off each item as you complete it.

☐ _____

☐ _____

☐ _____

☐ _____

☐ _____

Hand in completed list to teacher.

To-Do List

Name: _____

Date(s): _____

Check off each item as you complete it.

☐ _____

☐ _____

☐ _____

☐ _____

☐ _____

Hand in completed list to teacher.

Graphic organizers such as to-do lists are a good way to help monitor students' ability to complete work. Many different types of checklists can be incorporated into students' daily work routines.

Sample

To-Do List

Name: __Ron_____

Date(s): __Jan. 25-26_____

Check off each item as you complete it.

☐ __Social Studies Research_____

☐ __Fractions Sheet_____

☐ __Title Page_____

☐ __Science Questions_____

☐ _____

Hand in completed list to teacher.

Reading Period Practices

Read independently chosen material.

Record reading in Reading Record.

Write weekly response in Reading Record.

**Complete any required reading
(research, literature circles).**

Work on language activities.

What to Do When You Are Finished

Complete any other work you may have to do in another subject.

Do some personal writing.

Use computer time.

Catch up on some reading.

Visit the puzzle/problem centre.

Create a research project.

Programming

Behaviours alone do not ensure the success of small-group instruction. Programming is the key element. There are two parts of programming the teacher must consider when planning for small-group instruction:

1. the actual small group outcomes; and
2. the outcomes for the large group or remainder of students who are not under the teacher's direct guidance at the time.

Because the learning time has to be as beneficial for the independent students as it is for the group under the teacher's direct tutorage, a successful plan is an attempt to keep both groups involved in similar objectives or outcomes. Students in the small group do not feel they are missing out on something else if they see the remainder of the class engaged in similar topics. They are able to focus better on the small-group instruction. In this situation, goals and objectives are directed at assisting students to become proficient readers of non-fiction. The objectives set up for the class at this time are based on Holdaway's third and fourth processes of learning: *practice* and *performance*. During the small-group instruction time, other students are engaged in independent reading with a focus on non-fiction material.

The following process is useful for students who are not directly involved in the small-group instruction.

- Students have a ready supply of non-fiction material on hand to read.
- Students keep track of their personal reading through a recording log, and, once a week, write a letter to the teacher, relating their reading experiences.
- Students rate each book with an established rubric. The rating scale helps students develop personal tastes in their reading choices and demonstrates to them that their opinion has value.
- At the end of the month, students tally up the books and pages and write them on a record-keeping sheet for their portfolios.

The recording system not only helps students track their own reading, but it also provides the teacher with information about a student's reading habits. When students know there is an audience for their opinions, they are more likely to read with care.

CHAPTER FIVE

THE GUIDED READING LESSON

As the class is settling into independent non-fiction reading and working on projects as follow-up to activating lessons, the teacher can prepare for small-group instruction. Small-group instruction for non-fiction is based on the principles of the guided reading program. In their book, *Guiding Readers and Writers (Grades 3–6)*, Irene Fountas and Gay Su Pinnell define guided reading: "Guided reading usually involves small groups of students who are at a similar place in their reading development. These students demonstrate similar learning needs and process text at about the same level. At times, you may group students of mixed abilities who share a common learning need, such as how to read charts and tables in informational texts" (p. 216).

WHAT IS GUIDED READING?

Principles of the Guided Reading Lesson

- The guided reading lesson format is intended to be a starting point for students to engage effectively with non-fiction text.
- The small-group instruction is continually altered, adjusted, and reworked to fit the needs of students.
- With each new group, and each initial assessment, the format may alter but the basic structure will remain unchanged.
- The guided reading lesson is conducted with a small group of four to five students. It may be one period or a series of sessions directed by the teacher on a particular topic/skill or need. There may be between one to three sessions at a time for a group. Each session may last 30 to 45 minutes in length.

This fits in with Fountas's and Pinnell's research, which states, "Experience suggests it is better to work with a group over several consecutive days" (p. 207).

Guided Reading Structure

- Multiple copies of the guided reading task are on hand for each student.
- Students read the material independently in the group, so the material should be at an instructional level.
- At times, groups may be homogeneous in nature. Students may also be grouped according to needs. For example, if a group is struggling with the procedural nature of directions, then they will be selected for a specific lesson based on those needs.

Guided Reading at Work

- The teacher and students gather around a work area where the teacher assigns parts of the material to read. It may be a paragraph at a time for shorter pieces or several pages for lengthier material.
- During the reading time, the teacher observes and makes anecdotal notes on reading behaviours for each student.
- Once everyone has completed the assigned reading, the teacher directs a discussion.
- The teacher asks questions of the students, seeking out further information on each individual's knowledge of the text and the processes they used to acquire that information.
- The teacher also uses this time to point out to students various strategies that could be used and different features of the text that the readers may not have been aware of at the time.

Once the series of lessons is complete, the group is dissolved and another group is constructed. Throughout the year, students will be in many different configurations of groups, based on their needs.

SMALL-GROUP MANAGEMENT FOR GUIDED READING

Management is the key to any successful program run in the classroom. The teacher is managing time, resources, and individuals. The set-up is very important in ensuring success with the program. The biggest component of management is preparation: the collecting of materials appropriate to the required needs, and having sufficient copies. This may make some people hesitate, as it implies extra commitment, workload, and maintenance to an already heavy load teachers have to shoulder. However, the preparation is not as demanding as it may seem. Teachers should view it as pre-planning work.

In fact, most teachers are already doing most of it. Once all the preliminary work is completed, preparation is fairly minimal, and regular planning and maintenance are sufficient.

Resources

Materials

Obtaining materials for the guided reading program is the first priority. Teachers will require a collection of basic materials to begin the program and should continue to add material throughout the year. Many publishers are now developing materials for schools specifically related to guided reading. Unfortunately, many of these kits are expensive, so a collection may have to slowly grow over time.

Time

Time is also another factor to consider. All material must be reviewed prior to purchase to see if it meets the needs of students. Most publishers are willing to provide preview copies of their material. Searching catalogues, contacting publishers, previewing, and then ordering can take some time. In-services and dialogue with colleagues can be beneficial and time-efficient.

Teacher-Created Materials

Teachers may want to create their own resources, based on, or adapted from, existing materials. Magazine articles, textbooks, and newspapers are good sources. It is important to collect multiple copies of material, usually six copies, so that there are enough copies for a maximum group of students as well as a copy for the teacher. Since resource material is such a priority, teachers may want to start with the construction of their own material. In this book are samples of material that may be photocopied. They can be a starting point as teachers seek out other resources. These materials are useful to have on hand to get started right away while the teacher continues to look for further materials.

Lending Libraries

Some schools are creating guided reading lending libraries. Instead of resources being channelled into one room, schools collectively buy, share, and store material as a large group. There are many options to explore for acquiring materials and each school/teacher must decide which is the most feasible system for their needs.

Physical Space

There is also the physical space to consider. A place in the classroom should be set up as the location for the guided reading lessons. Whatever location is selected should be removed as much as possible from the regular flow of classroom traffic. A round table works well for the format. Educational companies produce horseshoe-shaped tables that allow the teacher easy access to all the students, with a good viewpoint.

Timetabling

Time is always a valuable commodity in the classroom. Timetabling for small-group instruction is a step requiring serious consideration. Guided reading should be incorporated into the existing program rather than being an additional component. Since the program design requires small-group work with the teacher's uninterrupted attention, the remaining students must be fully engaged at an independent level.

Record Keeping

With all the resources available and timetabling arranged, the next step is to develop a teacher portfolio for guided reading/small-group instruction. This portfolio will contain all records. The portfolio should be divided into two main parts. The first section contains individual records on each student, with a profile of them as a reader—their strengths, weaknesses, attitudes, learning, and their growth. The second half contains teacher notes related to the small-group instruction that occurs for each guided reading lesson. These notes are often referred to in later sessions or to assess the effectiveness of the instruction.

Individual Student Notes: For each student, the teacher may want to include the following pages as part of their profile: a reading interview/profile that each student fills out at the beginning of the year and then a second one mid-year; a record chart continuum related to specific skills; and anecdotal records. These records are maintained regularly throughout the year.

The use of a rubric is beneficial for keeping track of student progress on a continuum chart. The chart can be colour-coded for easy reference, related to the time of year. Progress charts, divided into three terms of approximately three months each, work well. For example, use red for the first term to shade in parts of the continuum of skills or write rubric numbers in red for knowledge of genre or use of features. In the second term, use blue to continue shading on the continuum and adding numbers on the charts. Finally, in the last term, use green to mark in progress during that time period.

In the anecdotal note section, the teacher records observations during the guided reading session. The teacher can easily flip back to session notes and refer to an observation at a later time.

At the beginning of the year, as students are growing accustomed to the routines and expectations, the teacher should begin with some initial evaluation. An Informal Reading Inventory about each student to learn more about their reading levels is helpful. A basic word-recall list and then a comprehension test provide useful information. Later on in the year, teachers may wish to do a follow-up with the reading inventories to chart reading progress.

Taking Notes During the Guided Reading Sessions: Before beginning a session with students, the teacher should explain to them that she/he will have a clipboard and papers on hand and will be taking notes during the session. The teacher explains to the students that this is a way to remember what was discussed during the guided reading session. It is important to explain this to students so that they do not feel any unnecessary anxiety.

It is also important to record notes as the group goes along, rather than trying to remember everything after the session. Students give many comments and insights during the session that reveal a great deal about them as readers. The students quickly grow comfortable with the teacher's note taking as they are going through text material.

A standard recording sheet during this time, listing all pertinent information, works best. If the students are provided with a worksheet during the reading session, have them keep the original in their Reading Record. Teachers may make a photocopy of a student worksheet to store in the profile section of their binder. Samples of these recording sheets and worksheets are provided on the following pages.

Guided Reading Student Profile

Student: _____

Guided Reading Rubric

0 – NS (needs support)   Does not demonstrate or display evidence of skill at this time. Requires teacher support with skills and information.

1 – INS (instructional)   Shows some knowledge of skills with teacher guidance, but not on a consistent basis. Makes attempts to work independently.

2 – DEV (developing)   Has knowledge of skill, can provide examples from text material, is beginning to work independently with accuracy.

3 – IND (independent)   Applies skills to own reading and tasks, uses skills to gain new knowledge, can explain their reasoning and thought process when engaging with text.

*NO (Not observed at this time)

Colour Code : | Term 1 | | Term 2 | | Term 3 |

Reading Skills	Date:	Date:
Decoding/Word Recognition Skills		
Comprehension Skills		

Knowledge of Genre (Non-Fiction)

	Date:	Date:	Date:
Instructional			
Explanatory			
Report			
Discussion			
Opinion			
Relate			

0 – NS   **1 – INS**   **2 – D**   **3 – IND**

Makes Use of Features (related to non-fiction)

Term	1	2	3		1	2	3
Bold print				Headings/subheadings			
Charts				Italicized words			
Diagrams				Maps			
Flow charts				Pictures			
Footnotes				Pronunciation guides			
Glossaries				Sidebars			
Graphs				Timelines			

Skills Continuum

Recognizes Cause and Effect	**0**	**1**	**2**	**3**

Compares and Contrasts	**0**	**1**	**2**	**3**

Sequences	**0**	**1**	**2**	**3**

Summarizes	**0**	**1**	**2**	**3**

Infers and Categorizes Data	**0**	**1**	**2**	**3**

Classifies and Categorizes Data	**0**	**1**	**2**	**3**

Distinquishes Fact from Opinion	**0**	**1**	**2**	**3**

Identifies Main Idea and Supporting Details	**0**	**1**	**2**	**3**

Materials Read by Student

Title	Date

Anecdotal Notes

STRUCTURING THE LESSON

In her book, *Guided Reading Basics*, Lori Jamison creates a structure that can be followed with each guided reading lesson. We have adapted her structure in these pages. Jamison states, "The guided reading lesson with informational text has the same form as that for narrative text. Before reading: book introduction to establish context and introduce key vocabulary. During reading: scaffolding students as they read. After reading: Revisiting the text to reinforce strategy use and extend learning" (p. 137).

The guided reading lesson for the small group also works in three sections, Pre-Reading, During Reading, and Post-Reading. A set of sheets based on this structure is included on the following pages, and can be used for the articles included in this book, as well as other forms, such as social studies texts, science material, and other non-fiction books.

Pre-Reading Activities
- teacher hands out copies of article and guided reading sheets
- group fills in the pre-reading section
- teacher highlights any specialized vocabulary students may need prior to reading
- group examines features in the article prior to reading

During-Reading Activities
- students engage in text while teacher records observations
- teacher may conduct mini-conferences with individual students at this time: asking students to read aloud a section; discussing what they are reading; offering reading strategies to individuals
- students generate questions as they read and record them on their guided reading sheets

Post-Reading Activities
- students complete the final section of their guided reading sheets through a small-group discussion of the text
- group discusses questions and answers, author's purpose and intent leading to genre identification, features that assisted reading, and helpful reading strategies
- teacher introduces follow-up sheets on reading strategies that further extend learning

Teacher's Recording Sheet

Guided Reading Session   Date(s): _____

Group Members: _____

Materials Used: _____

Focus:

Genre _____   Structure _____   Style _____   Elements _____

Notes: _____

_____

_____

_____

_____

_____

_____

_____

Guided Reading Student Worksheet

Guided Reading Group: _____

Date: _____

Title of piece of writing: _____

Pre-Reading

My predictions (what I predict the reading will be about): _____

_____

_____

_____

_____

Key words to know: _____

_____

_____

_____

_____

Features that may help me with the reading (maps, diagrams, titles, bold print, sidebars, pictures, headings, etc.): _____

_____

_____

_____

_____

_____

_____

_____

During Reading

Start reading. While you are reading, think of some strategies to use to help you understand the information. Record any questions that may come to your mind as you are reading.

Questions: _____

_____

_____

_____

_____

Post-Reading

What did you learn from the reading? _____

_____

_____

_____

_____

Were your questions answered after you finished reading? Were you left with any new questions?_____

_____

_____

_____

_____

What do you think the author's message (purpose or intent) was in writing this piece?

_____

_____

_____

USING INFORMATIONAL ARTICLES IN THE GUIDED READING LESSON

The next section contains reproducible articles for small-group instruction. These articles have been grouped according to non-fiction styles the teacher can use with the article. Students should be given copies of the guided reading learning sheets to use as graphic organizers as they read the article. Each student receives a copy of the article and an extended learning sheet.

Each non-fiction style has three separate articles that illustrate the theme. This format lets the teacher conduct several group sessions throughout the year related to the topic and discuss the content and non-fiction style. Each of the articles supports the previous mini-lessons related to genre, structure, style, and elements. As students read each article, they can identify these parts of non-fiction. The order of the styles is flexible so teachers can organize lessons based on the needs of the students. The following lists the articles included with each non-fiction style.

- Non-Fiction Style: *Cause and Effect*
  Extended Learning Sheet: Cause and Effect
  Articles: *Lake Disappears Overnight!*
             Tornadoes
             The Sinking of Titanic: *How It Changed the Course of History*

- Non-Fiction Style: *Compare and Contrast*
  Extended Learning Sheet: Compare and Contrast
  Articles: *Africa and the Arctic: Not as Different as They Seem?*
             Cats or Dogs? Choosing a Pet that's Just Right for You
             Team or Individual Sports: Which One Is for You?

- Non-Fiction Style: *Sequencing*
  Extended Learning Sheet: Sequencing
  Articles: *How to Make Your Own African and Arctic Artefacts*
             Bracelets with Messages
             From Wheat to Bread

- Non-Fiction Style: *Classifying and Categorizing Information*
  Extended Learning Sheet: Classifying and Categorizing Information
  Articles: *Lance Armstrong: More than Just an Athlete!*
             China: A Fascinating Land
             Celine Dion: Music Superstar!

- Non-Fiction Style: *Identifying Main Ideas and Supporting Details*
  Extended Learning Sheet: Identifying Main Ideas and Supporting Details
  Articles: *Dragonflies: People's Best Friend*
                Rollerblading: For Fun and Health!
                The World of Photography

- Non-Fiction Style: *Distinguishing Fact from Opinion*
  Extended Learning Sheet: Distinguishing Fact from Opinion
  Articles: *The Lost Atlantis*
                The Mystery of Oak Island
                Horoscopes: They're in the Stars

- Non-Fiction Style: *Summarizing*
  Extended Learning Sheet: Summarizing
  Articles: *Totem Poles: Giant Storytellers*
                The Grand Canyon: One of the Wonders of the World
                All About Horses

- Non-Fiction Style: *Inferring and Drawing Conclusions*
  Extended Learning Sheet: Inferring and Drawing Conclusions
  Articles: *The Curse of King Tut*
                The Bermuda Triangle: Fact or Legend?
                The Importance of Recycling

NON-FICTION STYLE: *CAUSE AND EFFECT*

"Cause and effect" is a relationship. When an event occurs, another action or event also occurs as a result of the first one. The cause is often the reason behind an event. Sometimes, many causes contribute to a single effect, or many effects may result from a single cause. Cause and effect are important concepts in non-fiction articles because they help to explain an idea.

As a reader, you can often identify a cause-and-effect relationship by some of the words used in the article. These are some of the more common words used in explaining a cause-and-effect relationship:

because of	is affected	is influenced
causes	produces	results in
is due to	when	if
the reason for	thus	therefore
consequently		

Extended Learning Sheet: Cause and Effect

List the event/action you are reading about.

_____

Cause	**Effect**
List all possible information explaining the causes	List all possible information explaining the effects

LAKE DISAPPEARS OVERNIGHT!

One night before you go to bed, you look out at a large lake near your village. The next morning it has vanished! Can this be true?

As hard as it is to understand, this strange occurrence actually did take place.

On the night of May 18, 2005, the Russian village of Bolotnikovo in the Nizhni Novgorod area had a large lake of a million cubic metres of water next to it. The lake stood some 300 metres away from the village. However, the next morning, all that was there was a large trench. Local fishermen came down to the lake that morning and were greeted with an enormous, muddy hole. The landscape around the forest's edge looked as if the water had been sucked in like a gigantic, unplugged bathtub. Trees were uprooted and sucked downward under the ground. Fishermen stared dejectedly, knowing this would mean much hardship for their livelihood. Village residents asked Russia's emergency services for help.

Specialists arrived at the site of the incident and examined the bottom of the lake, seeking possible victims. Luckily, there were no people near the lake when it was virtually emptied.

The chief of the local firefighting brigade said that a large number of trees had been sucked under the ground. "If a human being finds himself in the middle of such a disaster, there will be no chance for a person to survive."

An official from a nearby village believed that the lake had flowed into an underground river. "I think that the disappearance of the lake is due to a vault of a large underground

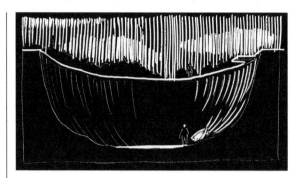

cave that connected with a river there. We believe that there is an underground river flowing here in the area, and the water of the lake has gone under the ground," he said.

Officials from the regional administration said that several houses went under the ground in the village of Bolotnikovo 70 years ago.

What Is a Sinkhole?

The lake in Russia disappeared into a sinkhole. What are sinkholes?

Sinkholes are common where the rock below the land surface is limestone, carbonate rock, salt beds, or rocks that can naturally be dissolved by groundwater circulating through them. As the rock dissolves, spaces and caverns develop underground. Sinkholes are surprising because the land usually stays intact for a while until the underground spaces just get too big. If there is not enough support for the land above the spaces, a sudden collapse of the land surface causes the sinkhole. These collapses can be small, or they can be huge and can occur where a house or road or even a lake is on the surface!

TORNADOES

What Are Tornadoes?

A tornado, also known as a twister, is a severe windstorm. You know it's a tornado when you spot a twisting, spinning funnel reaching down from a huge, dark cloud. The funnel looks like an elephant's trunk swaying back and forth. A tornado funnel can be 3 metres to slightly over 1.6 kilometres wide. Some funnels do not extend to the earth.

Others touch down and race across land. Still others skip or leap from one point to another. They touch down, plough a path of destruction, and then rise up into the air.

At the centre of the storm, tornadoes spin around at high speeds. Some twist and twirl at more than 480 kilometres an hour. Tornado winds are the strongest-blowing winds on earth.

Most tornadoes are white or clear in colour at first. They may even seem to shimmer in the light. When they touch the ground, the funnels turn black or dark grey as they sweep up tonnes of dirt, dust, and debris. Tornadoes are formed by a thunderstorm. Not all thunderstorms produce tornadoes. Scientists are not quite sure why some thunderstorms produce tornadoes and others do not. They do know tornadoes are formed when cold air meets warm air. They continue to explore other possibilities.

Traits of a Tornado

Tornadoes usually last less than one hour. Some die out in just a few minutes.

Sometimes groups of tornadoes will form at the same time. These tornadoes strike one after the other, creating stormy conditions for several hours. Often, a tornado's spinning funnel wind will make a shrill hissing or whistling noise that can be heard for kilometres around. Some people say the sound is like the buzzing of a million bees. When the tornado touches down and rips across the earth, the sound changes. The hiss becomes a loud, deafening roar that people compare to the noise of 100 jumbo jets taking off; others say it is like the sound of a speeding train rumbling through a tunnel.

When and Where You Find Tornadoes

Tornadoes can occur all year long, but most tornadoes happen between April and June, with the highest number in May. The fewest occur during December and January. Tornadoes can form at any time of day or night, but most develop late in the afternoon, the warmest time of the day. Most touch down between 4:00 and 6:00 PM.

Most tornadoes strike in the midsection of the United States and Canada. A stretch of land in the middle of the United States is known as Tornado Alley. States such as Texas, Kansas, Nebraska, Iowa, and Missouri have more tornadoes pass through them than anywhere else in the world. Thunderstorms form in Tornado Alley when cold air flowing across the Rocky Mountains meets warm air flowing up from the Gulf of Mexico. Only a few of the thousands of thunderstorms that form there produce tornadoes.

Damage Caused by Tornadoes

Each year, an average of 100 people are killed by tornadoes. Such winds can easily overturn trucks and destroy homes. The funnel cloud of a tornado sucks up everything it touches—dirt, crops, cars, water, animals, and people—and drops them farther along its path. Tornadoes have sucked up whole ponds with everything in them. When the tornadoes dropped the water, people thought it was raining frogs and fish! Sometimes a tornado seems to hop along its path. Such a tornado can tear one house to pieces and leave the house next door untouched.

What to Do if a Tornado Hits

Listen to the radio or TV for tornado watches and warnings in your area. A tornado watch means conditions are right and tornadoes might be coming! Stay tuned for more information. A tornado warning means tornadoes have been spotted. When this happens, go to your basement if you have one. If you don't have a basement, go to a closet or bathroom on the first floor of your house (a room without windows is best). Listen for an "all clear" message.

Amazing Tornado Facts!

In November 1915 in Great Bend, Kansas, a tornado hit. Some amazing things happened during that tornado. It blew a cheque all the way to Palmyra, Nebraska, a full 488 kilometres away, the farthest that a tornado has ever carried debris. It picked up 45,000 ducks and then rained them down to the earth. The tornado ripped off one wall of Grant Jones's grocery store but didn't disturb the cans and boxes on the shelves against the wall.

The tornado of June 1958 sucked a woman out of a window in her El Dorado, Kansas, home, carried her 18 kilometres and gently dropped her to the ground. The tornado winds of June 23, 1944, blew all the water out of the West Fork River in West Virginia for a few minutes. A tornado in the country of Bangladesh on April 26, 1989, left 1300 people dead. A tornado wiped out the town of Coatesville, Indiana (population 500), on the evening of March 26, 1948. Four out of every five buildings were destroyed and 16 people were killed.

THE SINKING OF *TITANIC*
How It Changed the Course of History

Many people are familiar with the story of the *Titanic*, the world's largest ship called "unsinkable," and its disaster on April 15, 1912, which killed more than 1500 people. The familiar story of how it hit an iceberg, causing the ship to sink, is only part of the complete story. What really could cause a ship claimed unsinkable to sink in three short hours? Why did so many people perish in the disaster? How did the sinking of the ship change the way all ships operate after that?

Unsinkable?

The *Titanic* was declared unsinkable because of its 16 watertight compartments. Even if one part should be struck by something, the remaining parts would keep the ship afloat. It was thought that the iceberg must have caused major damage to wreck so many of the compartments. In 1985, the *Titanic* wreck was located and diving crews were able to get new information about the sinking. Experts have since found evidence that it was *where* the iceberg hit the ship rather than *how hard* it hit that caused the damage. It was thought a large gash must be on the ship but no large gash was discovered. Instead, six small breaks, spread out along the hull, made holes in six of the watertight compartments that reached out along the seams of the metal. This has led to the question that perhaps the steel used in the *Titanic* structure was not as strong as it was thought to be. Tests have proven the steel could not stand up to strong impacts. Added to the problem was the fact that the *Titanic* was running in unusually cold waters for that time of year. With near-freezing temperatures, tests showed, the steel became extremely brittle. Later investigations also found that the ship was travelling too fast in such dangerous waters.

Lost Lives

The ship sank in three hours. Many people question why there was not enough time to get all the people off the ship. The boat had only enough lifeboats for about half the passengers and crew. When the announcement was made to go to the lifeboats, many people did not believe the message. They truly believed they were on an unsinkable ship. In the confusion that took place, many of the first lifeboats were not completely filled before being lowered into the water. Most of the passengers in the lower decks perished. They were still in the lower parts of the ship when it was too late to get out. Many of these passengers were immigrants who did not speak English and would not have understood the directions for getting to safety.

As there were fewer and fewer lifeboats, people started jumping overboard. However, these people did not last long in the cold waters of the northern Atlantic. If the ship had been in more southern waters, some people may have survived in the water by clinging to debris from the ship.

Rescue took longer than it should have. In fact, there was a ship nearby that the *Titanic* tried to signal with flares, but the ship, the *Californian,* did not respond. The radio operator had gone to sleep for the night and did not see the *Titanic*'s signals for help.

Because of this disaster, many changes were made to the operations of ships.

- *Titanic*'s sinking resulted in the formation of the International Ice Patrol to warn ships of ice conditions in the sea.
- The lanes used by ships were moved further south.
- It is now the law that ships have enough lifeboats for everyone on the ship.
- Ships must have 24-hour radio service.
- SOS became the international signal for calling for help.

NON-FICTION STYLE: *COMPARE AND CONTRAST*

When you compare two things, you are explaining how they are similar to each other. When you contrast two things, you are explaining how they are different from each other.

When you are reading to find comparisons and contrasts, certain vocabulary can help you locate the information. Here is a list of some compare and contrast words.

Compare Words	Contrast Words
like	unlike
same as	different from
similar	less
likewise	more
also	whereas
too	but
as does	instead
both	on the other hand
each, either/neither	"er" words such as drier, hotter

Extended Learning Sheet: Compare and Contrast

Use the graphic organizer below to record details about your two subjects. Where the circles overlap, write how the subjects are the same. The outer parts of the circle are used to record differences.

Subject: _____   Subject: _____

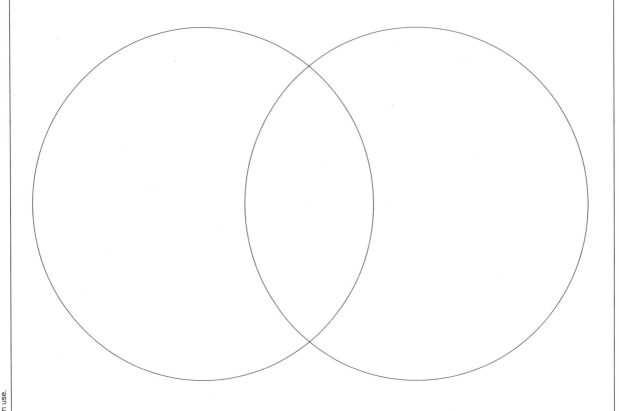

AFRICA AND THE ARCTIC
Not as Different as They Seem?

Africa is a continent composed of many countries. Our impression of it is as a dry, hot land. The Arctic is a northern region of the world also composed of different countries. Our impression of it is as an ice-packed, chilly land. They are two very different regions. Correct? After reading this article, you may think that the two are not as different as they may seem.

Climate

A country such as Zambia in Africa has a temperature in the 25 to 30 degree Celsius range all year, and a place like the Northwest Territories in Canada has -25 to -30 degree Celsius temperatures much of the year. However, they do have something in common! Many people would say both have extreme desert-like climates—the difference being that one is a hot desert and the other a cold desert. A desert is any piece of land that receives very little *precipitation*.

Examine the table of precipitation. As you see, a period of little precipitation occurs in each region at different times.

Precipitation in mm.	Zambia (rain)	N.W.T. (snow)
Jan.	236	10
Feb.	142	10
Mar.	18	8
Apr.	3	9
May	0	20
June	0	40
July	0	50
Aug.	0	45
Sept.	0	25
Oct.	10	22
Nov.	91	24
Dec.	150	15

On the other hand, there are some periods of heavy rainfall in each region.

The Land

Africa is a diverse land, which has the world's driest deserts and some of the most luxurious jungles. It has mountains with snow on the top and flat, dry, cracked land. The Arctic is composed of flat land with no trees. The Arctic is in an area called "above the treeline." In the Arctic it is too cold, and there is not enough yearly sunlight, for large trees to grow.

Homes

These days both areas have modern forms of homes. The traditional homes are the ones that give us the most information.

Inuit people of the Arctic made homes out of ice and snow blocks. The design was very practical. Its domed shape gave a strong foundation and kept heat inside. Very little furniture was found in the igloos. The Inuit could travel and hunt for their food and stop to make a home. This allowed them to move around with the animals they hunted.

The Zulu people of South Africa build homes known as beehive huts. The hut has a dome shape. The framework is made of flexible sapling branches staked to the ground and tied together with grass. Large mats are laid over the framework, like tiles, to keep the rain running off.

The Bedouin people of Africa are shepherd people who move around, always searching for pasture for their herds of animals. The homes they had were not permanent, either. They lived in tents. The tents are striped squares of tightly woven camel hair pegged down over poles and open at one end. There is very little furniture in them.

The beehive huts had shapes similar to the Inuit igloos. However, these homes were more permanent for the Zulu people.

The People

The Arctic people and the African people have many cultural differences, such as in their styles of clothes and languages. What they do have in common is their love of stories. Both groups have a long history of telling stories. These stories are passed on from generation to generation and are often entertaining tales that teach lessons.

We examined a few features about two interesting places in the world: Africa and the Arctic. If you do some further research, you will find even more features that make each place unique, but you will also find many more features they have in common. The two regions may not be as different as we think. What do you think?

The traditional igloo could be built in many different places, making it an ideal shelter for travelling groups.

Cats or Dogs?
Choosing a Pet That's Just Right for You

You have been thinking about it for a long while and now you are at the point of decision making—your family is thinking of getting a pet. Before you run out and get one, there are some important considerations. The number one question is, what type of animal will you get? There are many choices: birds, fish, and reptiles are some of them, but the two most popular and common choices remain cats and dogs. Let us examine these two choices more closely.

Because they are fur-covered animals, cats and dogs are the two most common pets that cause allergies in people. If someone in your house does have allergies, you may have to consider a different type of animal as a pet.

The type of personality you have may assist you in deciding which pet is for you. If you are a very affectionate person, if you need company around you often, or if you

are an active person, then a dog may be for you. Dogs enjoy lots of companionship. They want a great deal of attention and enjoy being petted and cuddled. Dogs also like to be active. Dogs require exercise each day, so be prepared to go for walks with your dog.

If you enjoy quiet and relaxation, if you like affection but don't need it constantly, then you're most likely a cat person. Cats do not require daily walks and enjoy spending time on their own, compared to dogs.

You also have to ask yourself if you have the commitment for a cat or a dog. Both animals live fairly long and will be with you for many years. The average lifespan of a small dog is 11 years and 12 years for a cat.

An animal needs a great deal of care. Cats do not require nearly as much attention as dogs. Cats will be comfortable spending the day at home alone. Cats spend

about 70 percent of the day sleeping and 15 percent of the day grooming.

In contrast, the first few months of training a pup can be nearly a full-time job. Exercise is important for dogs. Lack of exercise can cause dogs/puppies to exhibit destructive chewing behaviour because they become bored or are trying to burn off excess energy. Taking your dog/puppy for a 15- to 20-minute walk is a necessary job.

Let's look at the pros and cons for each animal.

CATS

Pros: Cats can be a perfect addition to a family that does not have the time required to give much attention to a dog. You do not need to worry about taking a cat for a walk. Cats can use a litter box, which can be helpful for those people who live in an apartment.

Cons: Cats may want to use your furniture as a scratch post for their nails. However, this can be prevented by getting your cat declawed. Some cats can shed to a great extent, so you will have fur all over your home. However, this can also be common with dogs. Cats can be dangerous around small babies, because they can jump, and may jump up into the baby's crib.

DOGS

Pros: Different types of dogs have a wider range of personalities compared to cats, so you are sure to find a dog that fits your family. Dogs will provide you with a great deal of affection, which is why they've acquired the name of "people's best friend."

Cons: Dogs can be very expensive. Not only can the initial cost of dogs be expensive, but vet bills will usually cost more than for a cat. Dogs need to be house-trained and require you to take them outside to relieve themselves. Dogs require more time commitment. Some long-haired dogs require daily grooming. Most dogs require a daily walk/run.

Whichever animal you do decide to choose as a pet, one thing both dogs and cats have in common is that they will provide you with many happy years as a pet owner.

TEAM OR INDIVIDUAL SPORTS
Which One Is for You?

There are many different kinds of sports in which you can get involved. You can get involved in more than one sport, but you can't do them all, so you do have to make some choices. Finding the right ones for you can take some time and you may want to try out quite a few sports before you settle on the ones you want to pursue. How do you decide which sport is for you? Learning about the sport, trying it out, will help. One other way that can help you make some first decisions is to decide which type of sport interests you the most.

There are two main types of sports: team sports or individual sports. When you play team sports, you become a member of a group working together. When you are involved in individual sports, you compete on your own against others. Some people enjoy team sports, while others prefer individual activities. Let's look at the differences and similarities between the two.

Team sports

Team sports allow you to be with friends and meet new people. In team sports, everyone is working together towards a common goal. This means you have to cooperate with others and learn how to deal with problems that might occur when there is a difference of opinion.

In a team sport, there is less attention on each individual's performance and more on the whole team's performance. If you are a person who does not like all the pressure of winning or losing to fall on your shoulders, then a team sport may be for you.

Being a member of a team can be hard for some people. If you are a member of a team, you may have to put your own ideas aside and go along with the team's ideas, even if you do not agree with them. In a team sport, you may want to keep the ball to yourself and be the one to score, but the right thing to do might be to pass the ball and let someone else score for the good of the team.

Individual sports

Individual sports attract people who would rather rely on themselves than others, and are very self-motivated. You measure your success by putting your skill up against other individual's. You try for a personal best through competition with others.

Individual sports are different in that the spotlight is on one person's performance and there is no one else to blame for losing. When there is success, you enjoy the full credit for the success. Some people find it is too much pressure on them to do individual sports because all the responsibility is placed on one person.

There are many instances where individual sports are practised in a team environment. For example, individual sports, such as swimming, running, gymnastics, and golf, may use team scoring in such events as relays.

Regardless of the sport, there are some things in common to most sports. Whether you are part of a team or going on your own, you will have to practise.

To be good at any sport, you have to be willing to put in the time to get better. If you choose to play a sport, you will have to become familiar with two things right away: sports have rules that you must follow; and all sports require some type of equipment.

Rules for any sport are different. It does not matter if it is a team sport or an individual sport, you have to become familiar with the rules. Once you know the rules, you can begin to attempt the sport.

You may not think all sports require equipment, but they do! Some sports, like hockey, require a great deal of equipment, while a runner may only require a good pair of running shoes. Gymnasts need mats and vaulting boxes, while a golfer needs clubs, balls, and tees.

Here is a list of some team and individual sports. Note: Some individual sports may include a partner or team at times.

Team Sports	Individual Sports	
basketball	gymnastics	swimming
hockey	tennis	running
ringette	martial arts	cycling
football	horseback riding	archery
soccer	figure skating	golf
volleyball	skiing	
baseball		

Can you think of any other sports that would fit in the lists?

NON-FICTION STYLE: *SEQUENCING*

Writing can be done in many different ways. The order in which the writer puts ideas down on paper is called *sequencing*. Sometimes sequencing is called *procedural* writing. Writers can choose many different ways to sequence their ideas. They can start in the past and work towards the present, or they can arrange ideas in the order in which the events happen. This is called *chronological* order.

Certain words can help you identify the sequence a writer chooses to use. Here are some of the more common vocabulary words related to sequence.

Sequencing Words	
after	next
before	then
numbers (firstly, secondly, thirdly) or the actual # symbol	preceding
following	prior
later	while
initially	when
finally	

Can you think of any others you might use?

Extended Learning Sheet: Sequencing

After reading your piece of non-fiction, think about the important information in it. Imagine you had to retell it to someone in the proper sequence. What would you say and what order would you use?

Topic	
First,	
Then,	
Next,	
After,	
Then,	
Next,	
Lastly,	

How to Make Your Own African and Arctic Artefacts
Make an Ajegaung (Holes and Pin Game)

Ajegaung is a game of skill traditionally played by Inuit people. Now you can make your own version of the game.

Object of the Game:
Tossing an object with holes in it into the air and catching it by one of its holes on a pin.

Materials:
Piece of rectangular lightweight wood (such as a strip of a shingle) or heavy cardboard; string; an unsharpened pencil; rubber band or tape.

Steps:

1. Cut your piece of wood (cardboard). The size and shape can vary a bit but it should be approximately the size of your hand. Your board should have a bit of weight when it is tossed in the air.

2. Prepare your wood (cardboard) with holes. They can be any size as long as the pin (pencil) can fit through them easily.

3. Have a piece of string ready (it should be approximately a ruler's length). Tie one end of the string through a hole in your wood and the other end to your pin. Fasten the string to the pencil with tape or a rubber band.

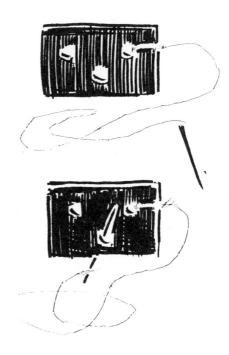

4. Hold the pin in your hand. Toss the wood into the air and catch it through one of the holes with the pin.

Make an African Rainstick

An instrument that creates the sounds of a summer rain shower, the African rainstick is made from a hollow tree trunk and filled with seeds, pebbles, and shells.

Materials:

Large cardboard tube (approximately 1 metre or 1 yard); various sizes of nails; hammer; cardboard; scissors; paint; masking tape; seeds; rice; beans; tiny shells.

Steps:

1. Hammer long and short nails into the tube in a spiral.

2. Cut two cardboard circles slightly bigger than the endings of the tube, then cut slits into it as shown.

3. Cover one end of the tube with the circle, fold down slits, and tape ends down.

4. Fill 1/10 of the tube with seeds, rice, beans, or small shells. Then, seal the other end with the second cardboard circle.

5. Decorate the rainstick by using paint, construction paper strips, markers, etc.

Flip and turn to make the instrument work!

BRACELETS WITH MESSAGES

Have you noticed more and more people with bracelets around their wrists? What you may be looking at is the latest trend: bracelets with messages.

For many ages, people have viewed bracelets as a decoration, a piece of jewellery worn around the wrist by females. Today, however, the bracelet is often more than just a piece of decoration. It is a way to share a message with other people and it is worn by both males and females.

One of the latest fashion trends has been the plastic coloured bracelet. Cyclist Lance Armstrong created the plain yellow plastic band as a fundraiser. Each one cost $1 and it was a way for people to support medical research for curing cancer. Millions of people began wearing them and soon the bracelets became so recognizable that people would immediately know you were showing your support.

Since Armstrong's yellow bands, known as Live Strong bracelets, came out, there have been others. You can find white ones showing support for peace, pink ones supporting breast cancer research, green ones supporting the environment, and multicoloured ones designed after national flags to show patriotism.

Bracelets with messages can be more than the familiar plastic bands. Many children who support charity groups have created a wide range of bracelets and sold them as part of fundraisers for disaster relief and special causes. Other people create bracelets to show their support for friends. These are most commonly known as friendship bracelets. So, the next time you are looking for a way to get involved with a cause or a group, think about wearing a bracelet with a message as a show of support.

MAKE YOUR OWN MESSAGE BRACELET

Now it's your turn to create a message bracelet. Here are some steps for making one type.

Materials:

9 to 12 clothespins; small beads

Instructions:

1. Bend open the clothespins carefully, and remove the springs without bending them.

2. Open the spring just wide enough to slip a small bead on each leg of the spring. You may want to use certain colours or even use alphabet beads to create a message.

3. Slide each of the legs onto the leg of another spring.

4. Continue adding beads and springs until the bracelet is big enough to fit around your wrist.

5. Fit the last spring in place on your wrist to secure the bracelet.

6. Use the leftover clothespins to make another craft!

FROM WHEAT TO BREAD

Do you know from which ingredients bread is made? You might say *flour*, and you are correct. It is the main ingredient in bread and other baking goods. Where does flour come from? Flour comes from a plant called *wheat*. Here is the story of how wheat turns into bread.

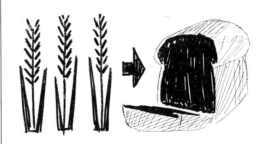

Wheat is a type of grass. It has been growing on our planet for over 10,000 years. Cultures from centuries ago used wheat for food. Today, wheat is the most widely grown cereal crop in the world —roughly 520 million tonnes are grown each year.

Wheat starts in spring with the farmer. The soil is ploughed to soften the earth for planting. The farmer spreads wheat seeds on top of the ploughed earth and then covers the seed with more soil to prevent the seeds from blowing away or being eaten by birds.

As the weeks pass, the seeds start growing and small roots begin to sprout. If the soil had not been ploughed, the small roots of the plant would have difficulty pushing down through the soil. The roots are important because they carry water to the rest of the plant and give strength to the plant to stand up.

Throughout the summer, the wheat plants grow until they are as tall as a young child! By late summer or early fall, the wheat plant is ripe for picking. The farmers use machinery to cut down the wheat. The combine harvester cuts off the stalks and the whole plant on top of the stalks is carried inside the machine. The stalks, called *straw*, fall onto the ground behind the machine and are collected in bales to be used for farm animals' beds. This is called *harvesting*.

Even though the wheat plant is very long, only a small part of it is used for making flour. The part used is the grain, which looks like a small seed. Machines separate the grain from the rest of the wheat plant. The grain is put into sacks and then shipped from the farm to different marketplaces. The wheat has to be properly cleaned before it can be milled. The wheat goes through several cleaning stages and tests before it is accepted. *Milling* is the process for turning the seed into flour. The wheat seeds are crushed by heavy rollers to make flour.

The flour is bagged and sent off to stores and bakeries. The next steps come from you when you decide to follow a recipe for baking. To make bread, flour is mixed with yeast, salt, and water, and then baked. It is a long process from those seeds planted in the ground to your table as delicious bread!

RECIPE FOR MAKING BREAD DOUGH CREATIONS

Ingredients:

1 envelope yeast	30 ml shortening
125 ml lukewarm water	30 ml sugar
5 ml sugar	1 egg beaten
750 ml flour	175 ml milk
5–7 ml salt	

Steps:

1. In a small bowl, dissolve 5 ml sugar in the lukewarm water. Sprinkle yeast on top and let stand until foamy (10–15 minutes).

2. Heat the milk in a large saucepan until bubbles start to form. Remove from heat and cool until it's lukewarm.

3. Add salt, shortening, sugar, and egg to the milk.

4. Add 125 ml of the flour and beat to form a smooth batter.

5. Add the foamy yeast mixture to the batter and beat until the mixture is smooth.

6. Add enough of the remaining flour to make a stiff dough.

7. Place the dough on a floured board and knead in the remaining flour. Keep kneading the dough until it is smooth (about 10–15 minutes).

8. Place the dough in a greased bowl, cover with a piece of waxed paper, and let rise in a warm place until it doubles in volume (usually 2–3 hours).

9. Cut a piece of dough and shape into long rolls, pretzel shapes, or create your own shape.

10. Place your dough shapes on a cookie sheet. Brush the tops with melted butter. Let them rise again, then bake. Bake at 190–200º C for about 15 minutes or until they are golden brown.

NON-FICTION STYLE: *CLASSIFYING AND CATEGORIZING INFORMATION*

When we learn about a subject, it is useful to organize the information. Often, we can group similar kinds of information under a subheading.

We do this is because it is easier to read and remember the information if we group together the facts that are related. When we go through information and group similar types of facts, we are classifying and categorizing.

A helpful tool for doing this is a web. For example, if we were classifying and categorizing information about an animal, on a web it might look like the one shown below, while the one on a famous person would be different. The number of categories depends on how you want to classify the information.

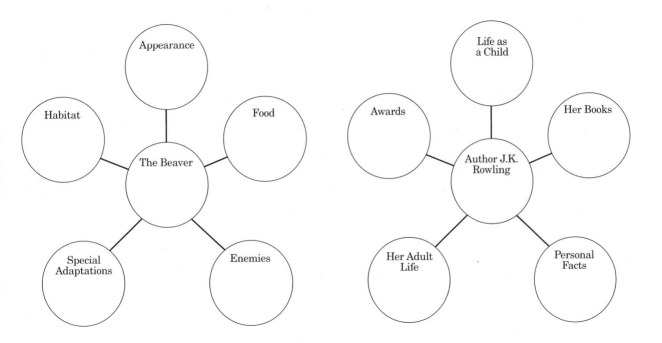

Extended Learning Sheet: Classifying and Categorizing Information

When you finish reading your article, go back through it and sort out the information into categories. Decide how you want to break up the information, and the title for your subheadings. Then record information into the proper spaces on the diagram below. Some spaces have already been provided, but you can create as many as you need.

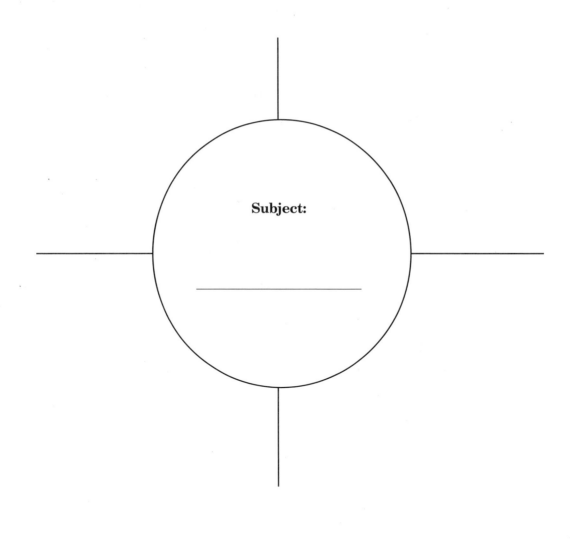

Subject:

_____

LANCE ARMSTRONG
More than Just an Athlete!

There are many great athletes and cyclist Lance Armstrong is one of them, but Lance is much more than an athlete; people view him as a model for hope and inspiration.

Lance was born in Plano, Texas, on September 18, 1971. When he was 13, Armstrong won the Kids Iron Triathlon. He later began entering triathlons (a *triathlon* is an athletic event made up of swimming, cycling, and running, in that order) for money, winning $20,000 when he was 15. As a high school senior, Armstrong qualified to train with the US Olympic team. He later made cycling his sport. In 1993 he won 10 titles and was called the "Golden Boy of American Cycling." After competing as a cycling amateur, winning the US amateur championship in 1991, and finishing 14th in the 1992 Olympics road race, Armstrong turned professional in 1992. The following year, he scored his first major victory as he rode solo to win the World Road Championships in Oslo, Norway. His successes continued with Team Motorola, with whom he won several classic one-day events. Also in 1995, he won the premier US cycling event, the Tour DuPont. He won the Tour DuPont again in 1996, and was ranked number one cyclist in the world.

But on October 2, 1996, Lance's life dramatically changed. He was diagnosed with cancer that was spreading to his lungs and brain. His doctors told him that he had a 40 percent chance of survival. The cancer could have meant the end of his cycling career, but Lance was determined to survive his cancer, never giving up. Ultimately, his cancer went into remission and he resumed his training. Many people doubted that he could return to his peak level as an athlete but Lance was going to prove them wrong.

In 1997, Lance returned to cycling, winning the Sprint 56K Criterium in Austin, Texas. That same year, Lance started the Lance Armstrong Foundation, a charitable organization that provides support for people with cancer. During the summer of 2004, the Lance Armstrong Foundation created the Live Strong wristband. The band was part of the Wear Yellow Live Strong program, to support cancer victims. Bands sold for only $1 each. Yellow was chosen for its importance in professional cycling. As of May 2005, over 50 million Live Strong wristbands had been sold.

Armstrong's true comeback came in 1999, when he won his first Tour de France. He won the race again in 2000, 2001, and 2002 to become the first American to win four Tours. He then won again in 2003 for five consecutive wins, and in 2004 he became the first cyclist to take the Tour for six straight victories. His 2005 Tour victory took place on July 24. Armstrong crossed the finish line to cheers of the public, for his seventh consecutive Tour de France win, setting records for total Tour wins and consecutive Tour wins.

The Tour de France is a long-distance road bicycle racing competition for professionals, held over three weeks in July in and around France. It has been held annually since 1903. The Tour de France is by far the most prestigious of all cycling competitions in the world.

A great deal of Lance's success has to do with his unique physical condition. Armstrong was born with a heart 30 percent larger than average, and his lungs have the ability to absorb twice as much oxygen as the average person. This means more oxygen-rich blood reaches his muscles, helping him use more energy and be less tired than his competitors. It is estimated that there are very few people with the same physical abilities.

Lance and his ex-wife had a son, Luke, shortly after his amazing come-back victory, and twin girls, Grace and Isabelle, two years later. After winning his seventh Tour de France, Lance Armstrong retired after a 14-year career. He stated he wanted to spend more time with his children as a major reason for retirement.

LANCE ARMSTRONG TIMELINE

1971   Born on September 18, in Plano, Texas. His mother, Linda, is 17 at the time.

1987   Competes in triathlons, making him a professional athlete at 16.

1989   Qualifies to train with the US Olympic developmental team.

1991   Becomes US National Amateur champion.

1992   Finishes 14th in the individual road race at the 1992 Barcelona Olympics.

1993   Wins 10 titles, including the US Pro Championship. At 22, is the youngest road racing world champion ever.

1996   Ranked # 1 cyclist in the world. Diagnosed with cancer, which has spread to brain and lungs.

1997   Marks his return to cycling by winning the Sprint 56K Criterium in Austin, Texas. Founds the Lance Armstrong Foundation.

1998   Marries Kristin Richard in Santa Barbara, CA, whom he met the year before while helping promote an Austin, Texas, race called the Ride for the Roses.

1999   Wins the Tour de France. Son Luke is born on October 12.

2000   Wins the Tour de France. Publishes *It's Not about the Bike*, about his comeback from cancer, which becomes a best-seller.

2001   Wins the Tour de France for the third straight year. Twin daughters, Isabelle and Grace, are born on November 20th.

2002   Wins the Tour de France, becoming one of five riders who have ever won four Tours de France.

2003   Wins a fifth Tour de France in five years. Only Spain's Miguel Indurain has five straight wins. Divorces wife Kristin Richards. Publishes another best-seller, *Every Second Counts*.

2004   Begins dating singer Sheryl Crow. Helps launch the Live Strong campaign, a fundraiser supported by the sale of millions of yellow bracelets. All proceeds go to support cancer survivors. Wins a sixth Tour de France, making him the most successful Tour de France rider ever.

2005   On April 18, announces he is retiring from professional cycling after the 2005 Tour de France. Wins his seventh and final Tour de France on July 24.

CHINA: A FASCINATING LAND

China is a remarkable country. You will find many books filled with fascinating information about this great country.

China is big in many different ways. It is the world's third-largest country by area (after Russia and Canada) and the largest by population. With a population of over 1.5 billion people, more than one-fifth of the world's total population lives in China.

China has many neighbours. The countries of Mongolia, Russia, North Korea, Vietnam, Laos, India, Bhutan, Nepal, Pakistan, Afghanistan, Tajikistan, Kyrgyzstan, and Kazakhstan all share borders with China. China also has more than 3400 islands as part of its land.

China's land is mainly mountainous. Mountains and hilly land make up 65 percent of the total area. China's higher *elevations* are found in the west, where some of the world's highest mountain ranges are located. There are five main mountain ranges in China. *Plateaus* are found in the southwest area, while *steppes* are found in the north and central parts of China. These different landforms can also affect the climate.

The climates of China are similar to the *continental* regions of the United States; mild temperatures occur alongside areas of desert and semi-tropical climates as well as snow-covered areas. Since it is such a large country and because of its physical features, many different kinds of climate occur within the country. The Asian *monsoon* greatly affects China's climate. In winter, cold, dry winds blow from Siberia, bringing low temperatures to all regions in the north and *drought* to the rest of the country. In summer, warm, moist air flows in from the Pacific Ocean, creating large amounts of rainfall in the form of *cyclonic* storms.

China is considered to have a very ancient culture. Its recorded history dates back nearly 4000 years, and may even go further back than that. China has had an organized government since the establishment of the Shang *dynasty* about 1766 BC, making it one of the oldest nations on earth. The Chinese were ruled by various dynasties for centuries. When a new dynasty was to come into power, it would overthrow the existing dynasty. On October 1, 1949, the People's Republic of China was formally established, switching the system of ruling dynasties.

When the new government was established, tourism was not encouraged so it was difficult for people to visit this fascinating country. Recently, China has allowed more visitors into its nation and people have been able to see many things.

Perhaps one of the most impressive sights in China is the Great Wall of China, also known as the Great Wall of 10,000. It is an ancient Chinese *fortification* built from the end of the 14th century until the beginning of the 17th century, during the Ming Dynasty, in order to protect China from raids by the Mongols and Turkic tribes. The wall spans over 6350 kilometres. It is the longest structure ever built in the world. Many stories have surrounded it, including the idea that the Great Wall is visible from space with the naked eye (which is not true).

China is home to many inventions. Some of the greatest inventions in the world were made by the Chinese. In the Tang dynasty, fireworks were invented; in the Han dynasty, they invented the wheelbarrow. The Chinese first *manufactured* the 'fan', invented spaghetti, and were the first to create kites. They invented the first object for counting, called an abacus, and invented paper and printing.

All this information is only the beginning of what you can learn about this country and its people. If you are interested in learning more about China but can not actually visit it, then head to your local library and find the next best thing—a book about this interesting place.

Glossary

Continental: of, or relating to, or characteristic of a continent

Cyclone: an area of low pressure, around which winds blow counter-clockwise in the northern hemisphere. Also the term used for a hurricane in the Indian Ocean and in the western Pacific Ocean

Drought: an extended period where water availability falls below the requirements for a region

Dynasty: the reign of a specific royal family for a period of time

Elevation: distance of something above a specific point (such as sea level); e.g., "there was snow at the higher elevations"

Fortification: defensive structure consisting of walls or mounds built around a stronghold to strengthen it

Manufacture: to put together out of components or parts

Monsoon: name for seasonal winds, especially in the Indian Ocean and southern Asia; a temperature-driven wind arising from the difference in heat between a land mass and the ocean

Steppe: a vast, semi-arid, grass-covered plain as found in southeast Europe and Siberia

Plateau: a relatively flat highland

China Quick Facts

Area: 9,571,300 sq km (3,695,000 sq mi)

Anthem: "The March of the Volunteers"

Capital City: Beijing

Official Language: Mandarin Chinese

Largest Cities:
Shanghai 9,480,000
Beijing 7,000,000
Tianjin 5,770,000

Currency: Yuan

Major Rivers: Yangtse, Yellow, and Pearl

Flag: China's flag is red with five golden-yellow stars.

Mountain Ranges: The highest mountain range in the world, the Himalayas, borders China. Other major mountain ranges in China are the Ch'ang-pai Mountains, the Tsinling Mountains, and the Nan range.

Animals: China has a great variety of wildlife, more than 100 rare species of the world, including the giant panda, the golden monkey, the white-lipped deer, the South China Tiger, the white-flag dolphin, the Chinese alligator, and the crowned crane.

CELINE DION—MUSIC SUPERSTAR!

Celine Dion is one of the biggest stars in pop music history. She is known throughout the world for her music. She has sold more than 100 million albums. Dion was born March 30, 1968, in Charlemagne, a small town 30 kilometres east of Montreal in the province of Quebec, Canada. Celine is the youngest child in a family of 14 children. Her parents were both musicians and ran a small nightclub. On weekends, the entire family performed and entertained for the customers. From her earliest age, people recognized that Celine had a voice that the public would love. At the age of 12, she wrote one of her first songs, which she recorded. Her mother and brother sent a copy of it to a manager. The manager would become someone very important in Celine Dion's life. He helped her become the musical superstar she is today and he also became her husband.

Celine has received all kinds of honours throughout her career. In 1983, at the age of 15, she became the first Canadian to have a gold record (a record that has sold close to 500,000 copies) in France and won a gold medal at a Japanese songwriting competition.

Even though Celine received these honours early in her life, it was in 1990 that her musical career really began. Her first record was released in the United States and became very popular. It would soon lead to many more songs, including "Beauty and the Beast," for the movie of the same name. Celine continued working hard to be successful, but another year was very important for her that was not related to music.

In 1994 she married her manager, Rene Angelil, in Montreal. After her marriage, Celine continued to achieve great things in her career. In 1996, her album, *Falling into You*, became the best-selling album of the year, topping the charts in 11 countries, and was voted Album of the Year at the Grammys, the highly honoured music awards. That same year Celine was invited to sing at the opening ceremonies of the Atlanta Olympics. Just when it was thought that Celine could not do anything greater, she recorded her most successful song of all: "My Heart Will Go On." It was the theme song for the movie, *Titanic*, the most popular movie of all time. The song became one of the most recognized songs throughout the world. In 2004 the music industry gave Celine the Diamond Award for selling so many records. She was only the second artist in history at that time to receive the award.

Celine's home country did not forget her, either. She was appointed an officer of the Order of Canada. The Order is a tribute from the Queen of England to Canadians who exemplify "the highest qualities of citizenship and whose contributions enrich the lives of their contemporaries." She has also been given the Order of Quebec title and placed on Canada's Walk of Fame.

But, with all her honours and success, there was one thing Celine wanted more than anything, and which she had trouble getting. She wanted to start a family with her husband but was having difficulty becoming pregnant. Finally, in January 2001, with the help of doctors, Celine was able to give birth to her son, Rene Charles, who, she says, is her greatest joy.

To stay close to her family, Celine decided that she did not want to be always travelling around the world, performing concerts. She decided to do weekly shows in the city of Las Vegas for three years. Celine was paid $100 million for all her performances.

Although Celine has very little spare time, she does enjoy doing things other than singing. Most of her time is spent raising her son. Recently, she took up the hobby of golf. She has enjoyed it so much that she and her husband bought their own golf course in Montreal. One of Celine's other passions is collecting shoes. She owns over 400 different pairs! Celine and her husbond Rene also try to get involved in other businesses. They own a number of 50s-styled restaurants across Canada called Nickels. Celine started her own beauty line, including a set of perfumes, and looks forward to creating more products.

Celine feels she has been very fortunate to be able to do what she loves and to be so successful at it. It is the reason why Celine has supported so many special charities and tries to help the unfortunate whenever she can. Celine regularly donates money to such groups as the T.J. Martell Foundation for cancer treatment and the Diana Princess of Wales Memorial Fund, which helps victims of war. Celine donated one million dollars to people in New Orleans who lost their homes from a hurricane named Katrina. Celine also donates money from concerts. She has given money to UNICEF for tsunami relief.

The one group that Celine has supported the longest is the Canadian Cystic Fibrosis Foundation. Celine has given money to the group, gives speeches for them, and assists the group in any way she can. This group is very special to

Celine for a very personal reason. Celine's niece, Karine, died from the disease at age 16. She died in Celine's arms and, from that moment on, Celine vowed to do whatever she could to help find a cure for the disease.

Celine continues to do what she loves the most—sing—and that is why she remains a true singing superstar.

Learn More About Celine

Height: 1.71 m (5 feet 7.5 inches)

Favourite Sports:
Golf and waterski

Favourite Singer:
Barbra Streisand

Favourite Number:
5 (named her chain of restaurants, Nickels, after a lucky 5-cent piece she found

Favourite Perfume:
Chanel no. 5

NON-FICTION STYLE: *IDENTIFYING MAIN IDEAS AND SUPPORTING DETAILS*

A paragraph is made up of sentences related to a certain topic. When authors write, they have an idea in mind that they are trying to convey. This is the main idea, the most important piece of information the author wants you to know. Details support the main idea by telling how, what, when, where, why, how much, or how many.

Finding the main idea and supporting details helps you understand the message the writer is trying to share with you.

Every paragraph has a main idea. It may be stated at the beginning of the paragraph, in the middle, or at the end. The sentence in which the main idea is discussed is the topic sentence of that paragraph. Although the topic sentence may appear anywhere in the paragraph, it is usually the first sentence. This sentence serves as a reminder for the reader about the main idea.

To identify the main topic, keep asking yourself, "What is this about?" You will soon find yourself repeating the same idea—this probably is your main topic. Sometimes you can spot the topic by looking for a word or two that is repeated. Usually, you can say what the topic is in a few words.

Extended Learning Sheet: Identifying Main Ideas and Supporting Details

Subject:

The main idea is ...

Supporting Information

Additional questions I have

DRAGONFLIES
People's Best Friend

Dragonfly: An Eating Machine

Many people see these flying insects and are afraid of them, due to their size. Even the name may sound frightening. But what if someone told you these insects may be your new best friend? What would make a dragonfly a friend to people? First, dragonflies do not harm people. They do not bite them or have any interest in people. In fact, dragonflies help us get rid of those insects that do bite us: mosquitoes and blackflies. Dragonflies are true eating machines and that's why they are our friends. A dragonfly will eat 300 to 600 mosquitoes a day. So you might want to welcome those flying giants rather than shooing them away.

Has 12,500 lenses per eye; near 360-degree vision, can see its prey as far as 36 metres away

Has wing beats of 30 per second; can reach speeds of 50 km/h; excellent flier; can change directions quickly and stop in mid-air

Pushes prey into mouth with legs; can consume enough food to match its body weight in 30 minutes

Uses its six bristly legs to create a basket trap and sucks mosquito to mouth in mid-air

You may see a large insect that you think is a dragonfly, but it might not be one—it could be a damselfly. The damselfly is related to the dragonfly and munches mosquitoes, but they do have slight differences in appearance. The chart below lists some of the differences.

	Dragonfly	**Damselfly**
Flight	Strong and fast	Flutters; slower
Eyes	Touch on top of head	Separated
Wings	Fore and hind wings different shape; at rest, wings are away from body	Fore and hind wings similar shape; at rest, wings are held together

ROLLERBLADING
For Fun and Health!

Rollerblading, also known as in-line skating, has become very popular in recent years. One of the main reasons so many people are taking up the sport is because it is an excellent way to get healthy and stay in shape.

Rollerblading is a sport you can take up with very little gear. All you need are the rollerblades (which are becoming reasonable in price); elbow, knee, and wrist pads; and a helmet. Anybody can try out this sport and do it at their own pace. Another reason why it is such good exercise is because you can do it almost anywhere! Since you do not require a lot of equipment, you can pack your skates with you when you go on a trip and rollerblade anywhere to get your exercise.

Many people believe in-line skating is better for them than running or aerobic[1] classes. When you do extreme running or jumping, the pounding of your feet on a hard surface can start to hurt the joints, such as your knees and ankles, that feel the impact. With in-line skating, you have the exercise but without the pressure on your joints. You might notice when you pick up speed that you will breathe faster and more often. That's because you are working aerobically. If your aerobic capacity is weak, you'll huff and puff at a higher speed. That's okay. It means you are getting a good workout.

Rollerblading can help you burn up extra calories that cause weight gain. In-line skating has been proven to burn as many calories as running. You can burn as many as 966 calories in one hour while having fun!

Rollerblading also helps you strengthen your upper leg, hip, and back muscles. The more you skate and the faster your pace, the stronger these muscles will become.

Rollerblading often helps you get involved in other sports. In-line skating is

[1] Aerobic: (are-O-bik) exercise. "Aerobic" means "with oxygen." In reference to exercise, the term refers to the intensity and duration of activity and the energy fuel being used.

used by many athletes to help them train for other sports. The muscles that are built up help these athletes run, jump, and move in other sports. So you may take up rollerblading and find you have increased ability to try another sport.

Another positive feature about rollerblading is that it can help you reduce stress in your life. Having a bad day? Worried about something? Put on your rollerblades, glide down the street, and you can forget your worries for a time. Skating for half an hour to an hour three times a week will definitely help you get into shape while you are having fun.

Safety and Protection

Safety and the proper equipment are important parts of rollerblading. Protection is required whether you're a beginner or a champion.

- The most frequent injury in-line skaters suffer is with the wrist. Wrist guards are so important because if you fall, your first reaction is to stick out your hands to help prevent the fall.

- A helmet is also a must because the head is so easy to injure and it is the most important part of your body.

- Pick surfaces that are fairly even without many cracks in the pavement. These cracks often lead to falls.

Tips for Starting to Rollerblade

- Before buying a pair of in-line skates, rent a pair and try them out, you'll see if you really enjoy the sport and if the skates are comfortable.

- Practise on grass or carpet before moving onto the pavement.

- Take professional lessons if you wish.

- To achieve good balance, stand with your feet side by side, arms slightly in front of you, ready to take a fall, knees slightly bent.

- The next important step to learn is how to stop. Each skate has a brake device attached on the heel of the skate. The idea is to slowly switch from your legs to your heel so that the brake pad rubs against the pavement and slows you down.

- Before you start going down hills, learn to brake on a flat surface.

- Recommended places to start rollerblading are in empty parking lots, tennis courts, basketball courts, or small, quiet streets.

THE WORLD OF PHOTOGRAPHY

Millions of people around the world have cameras and take pictures. At most special occasions and on holidays, you will find someone snapping pictures. Photography can be a wonderful hobby and there is much you can learn about the subject. Here are some tips for starting the hobby of photography.

One of the first points to discover is what kind of photography interests you. There are many different subjects that interest people and some photographers can spend their entire lives working at one particular subject. The best thing to do is to start looking at different kinds of pictures. Your local library will have a photography section. Many books feature the work of different photographers and their subjects. Some people view their photography as art, while other photographers use it for personal reasons or as a business (many photographers will sell their pictures for postcards, calendars, etc).

Some Subjects in Photography

- animal/wildlife
- landscape
- people
- flowers/plants
- sports
- travel
- abstract art
- fashion
- weather

Get the Right Equipment

Once you have some idea of what interests you, then you need to start looking for your equipment. The first piece of equipment to get is your camera. Even this can be a tough choice. Do you want to use a digital or film camera? Talk to camera experts and explain your purpose. What subjects do you want to photograph? They can help you decide which camera is best for you. After you have your camera, many other pieces of equipment will assist you with your picture taking. These are called *accessories*. The type of photography you do will help you decide which accessories you need.

Some accessories, like a tripod or a camera bag, are considered essential for almost all photographers, while others, like a wireless remote, are for special types of photography, and most camera users will never have a need for them. Even the type of film you use in your camera will depend on the type of pictures you plan to take.

Start Shooting

One of the best ways to learn more about photography is to get out and start taking pictures. You will soon begin to learn from mistakes you make and things you do right. Look at the pictures you take to see what is right and wrong about the picture. When you take more pictures, make adjustments to what you did before. There are many different ways of taking pictures. These are called *techniques*. As you practise picture taking, you will become more familiar with techniques.

Continue Learning

There is a great deal of help out there for the photographer. As you start taking more pictures, continue to build on your knowledge of the subject. You can find courses, books, videos, and magazines that will offer you all the tips you need.

Some Basic Techniques

Contrast A light subject will have more impact if placed against a dark background and vice versa.

Depth of Field This is the area or "zone" of a photograph, from front to back, which is in focus.

Balance Placing the main subject off-centre and balancing the "weight" with other objects will be more effective than placing the subject in the centre. Informal balance is considered more pleasing in a photograph than symmetric subjects.

Framing A "frame" in a photograph is something in the foreground that leads you into the picture or gives you a sense of where the viewer is placed.

Rule of Thirds This is based on the idea that the eye goes naturally to a point about two-thirds up the page. Also, by visually dividing the image into thirds (either vertically or horizontally), you achieve the informal balance mentioned above.

NON-FICTION STYLE: *DISTINGUISHING FACT FROM OPINION*

When you are reading, how can you tell if the information you are given is a fact or an opinion?

Facts are statements that can be verified, which means you can check the information elsewhere and find it stated as truth. Opinions are statements based on the author's personal belief.

Sometimes, an author can make such an excellent use of facts to help support their opinions that you are not sure whether what you are reading is fact or opinion. When an author does this, they are creating support for their argument.

Facts are information. They can be found in all types of non-fiction. Some of the most common documents that make use of facts are official government and legal records, science texts, and reference books, such as encyclopedias, atlases, and textbooks. Facts may be expressed in written form, but they are often recorded as numbers or quantities, weights, dates, and measures.

Opinions usually use information that cannot be measured or proved. Opinions often use general words, such as *large amount* or *many* or *few*. It is difficult to get exact information from opinions. Opinions represent one viewpoint on a topic. Opinions also place a value on an idea, stating that one viewpoint may be better than another.

Extended Learning Sheet: Distinguishing Fact from Opinion

Use this chart to distinguish fact from opinion. Examine an article you have just finished reading. Decide which information is fact and which information would be considered opinion. List all facts in the Fact Column and all opinions in the Opinion Column. Be prepared to explain why you think a statement is a fact or an opinion.

Fact Column	**Opinion Column**
_____	_____
_____	_____
_____	_____
_____	_____
_____	_____

THE LOST ATLANTIS

The story of Atlantis has been around for thousands of years. The most-asked question about Atlantis is whether the story is true or just imagination.

About 11,000 years ago, there was an island in the middle of the Atlantic Ocean with a large population. The people were wealthy, because the island had many natural resources. The rulers of this island ruled over people well into Europe and Africa. The island was Atlantis.

Atlantis was the kingdom of Poseidon, god of the sea. When Poseidon fell in love with a human woman, he created a home for her at the top of a hill in the middle of the island and surrounded it with rings of water and land to protect her. At the top of the hill a temple was built to honour Poseidon, which housed a giant gold statue of him riding a chariot pulled by winged horses. It was here that the rulers of Atlantis would come to discuss laws, pass judgments, and pay tribute to Poseidon. A water canal for travel was cut through the rings of land and water. The city of Atlantis lay outside the outer ring of water, where most of the people lived.

The climate was such that two harvests were possible each year, one in the winter and one in the summer. The lands had mountains, which soared up to the sky. Villages, lakes, rivers, and meadows were found along the mountainsides. The island gave all kinds of herbs, fruits, and nuts to the people, and all kinds of animals, including elephants, roamed the land.

For ages the Atlanteans lived simple, peaceful lives, but slowly they began to change. Greed and power began to corrupt them. When Zeus, the king of the gods, saw this, he decided a punishment was necessary. In one giant surge, it was gone. The island of Atlantis and its people were swallowed up in the sea.

This story was told by Plato over 2000 years ago in his books *Timaeus* (tîmê'us) and *Critas* (kritêus). Plato was a philosopher/teacher of the time. His writings are the only known accounts of Atlantis. They have been part of a debate for over 2000 years.

Many people believe the tale to be fiction, part of Plato's imagination, used to teach a lesson. Others believe that the story was inspired by a true catastrophe and is an accurate account of a long-lost land.

People who believe the story of Atlantis is a true account have been creating theories for thousands of years as to the location of Atlantis.

Some believe Atlantis is located around the Azores Islands. The Azores are a group of islands located about 1500 kilometres off the Portuguese coast. Some people believe the islands are the mountaintops of the sunken continent of Atlantis.

Other people believe Atlantis was an exaggeration of the historical destruction of the island of Thera, also known as Santorini. Thera is a volcanic island located north of Crete in the Aegean Sea. Some time around 1500 BC, it was devastated by a volcanic explosion. Artefacts found on the island indicate an ancient culture did inhabit the island. Others say the dates of Plato's story for Atlantis do not match up to the actual event on Thera and the island could not be Atlantis.

There have been dozens—perhaps hundreds—of locations proposed for Atlantis.

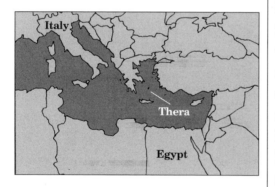

Some are scientific attempts to solve the mystery, while other theories are based more on legend.

Some researchers believe the present-day Antarctica could have been ancient Atlantis. Their idea is known as "earth crust displacement." An examination of the size of Plato's lost continent forms the basis of the work. This theory has some scientific fact. Because the earth is known to wobble on its axis over thousands of years, the South Pole could, at one time, have been at the equator. We also know that Antarctica is a series of islands covered with ice to create a single continent. When the South Pole froze over (due to the wobbling), the city would have been covered with ice. The ancients may have thought that it sunk when they could not find it.

A few people have said Atlantis is the southern part of Finland, where a small group of people lived during the Ice Age. Some have placed the location of Atlantis between Britain and France. Others believe the island of Atlantis is Ireland. They say similarities of both size and landscape are significant.

Robert Sarmast, an American architect, claims to have definitely found the lost city of Atlantis on November 14, 2004, saying that by using sonar scans he was able to find human-made walls that matched the description of the structures described by Plato. The site lies 1500 metres deep in the Mediterranean Sea between Cyprus and Syria. Several geologists were quick to dispute the claim, as the place was deep under water during the period in which Atlantis was said to have existed.

Others say Atlantis was never found because we have all been looking in the wrong places. Fact or fiction? What is your opinion?

THE MYSTERY OF OAK ISLAND

Oak Island is a 140-acre island located in Mahone Bay, just off the eastern coast of Nova Scotia, Canada.

At first it may seem like any other uninhabited island, but, in fact, it is the site of one of the world's greatest treasure hunts. For over 200 years, adventurers have come to this island in search of treasure. They believe someone came to this island long ago and buried something. Exactly who they were and what they buried remain unknown to this day. Yet, millions of dollars have been spent searching for the treasure and some people have even lost their lives in the search. The believers say there is enough evidence to point to fabulous treasure. Others say it is part of imagination and have named the diggings the Money Pit.

The mystery of Oak Island started in 1795 when a 16-year-old Nova Scotia boy was exploring the island. He found a large hole in the ground just below an oak tree. It seemed as if someone had dug a hole and filled it in again. He returned with friends and started digging. Little more than a metre down, they found a layer of stones uncommon to the island. Then, three metres down, they found a platform of oak logs close together in the walls of the shaft. Below the oak platform, they found more earth. At six metres, they found another oak platform, and another at nine metres. The pit was so deep that the boys could not remove the logs and gave up for the time.

In 1803 the boys returned to the island with a wealthy businessman who could hire a group to dig even further. The group found more oak platforms, one every three metres. At 30 metres, they discovered a large, flat stone with a message engraved in code. It was translated to mean "Forty feet below two million pounds are buried."

The workers removed the rock and platform and kept digging. But, at this point, water started to fill the hole. By the next day, the pit was completely filled with water. They tried removing the water but could not do it. The water kept filling the hole. The group tried digging a new hole around the existing one, but every time they got close to the original hole, water would return. The group eventually gave up. In 1849 a new group tried to get to the bottom of the pit. They used modern machinery and soon hit a spot of oak and loose metal pieces. Three small pieces of metal and wood were brought to the surface and this group believed two chests were down in that pit.

But, every time they dug, the water filled the pit like a drain. The pit filled

with water at a rate of 600 gallons per minute.

In 1861 a new group came to the island and tried to drain the pit. They too failed. Over the next century, many more attempts were made to retrieve the treasure. Every group failed. By now, the Money Pit had so many holes dug around it, the puzzle was growing in difficulty. In 1965, four people drowned in the Money Pit when they fell into the water of the shaft.

Today there are people still convinced that the treasure exists, but the searches have been fewer as many people think it is hopeless to solve the mystery and collect the treasure. Others are still curious. Who is responsible for creating such a clever trap and what could the treasure possibly be? There are many different ideas as to who is responsible and what the treasure may be. Some of the ideas have included those below.

Captain Kidd. The notorious pirate. Legends exist about his secret stashes of treasure buried by him and his crew. People believe maps still exist showing some of Kidd's treasures. Some people believe Oak Island is one such location.

Francis Bacon. Many people believe that William Shakespeare's famous plays were not written by him, but by someone else. Francis Bacon is that person. Since the original scripts of Shakespeare's plays have never been found, the idea is Bacon buried them somewhere to be found in the future. Some believe the resting place is Oak Island.

The French. Some people believe the French buried money on the island to hide it during the battles with the English when the Americas were being settled.

The Vikings. Nearly a thousand years ago, the Vikings did travel to this area. Some people say they had something so important to hide that they built the shaft system to hide it. However, it is unknown what the Vikings could have had that would have been so valuable that they would set up such a system to hide it.

Stranded Spanish ship. Some people say it is possible that a Spanish ship from hundreds of years ago was returning with gold and jewels from Central or South America and went off-course. Nearly shipwrecked, they stopped at Oak Island, hid the treasure while repairing the ship, and planned to return later for it.

British. This theory is similar to the French theory except that it may be royal jewels hidden beneath Oak Island.

Inca or Maya treasure. The Inca people had great wealth. Much of their wealth disappeared. Some people believe that a group of Incas or Mayas from South America came and buried their wealth on Oak Island to keep it out of the reach of their enemies.

No such treasure. Many people are convinced there is nothing valuable in the bottom of the Money Pit. While they agree there is some sort of system that was built here, nothing so valuable was left in the bottom and, if it did exist, it is long gone by now.

What do you think could be the mystery of Oak Island?

HOROSCOPES
They're in the Stars

For centuries, people used horoscopes or astrology as a way to foresee future events or learn secret knowledge through **omens** (signs that are believed to hold information about the future). Today, not many people believe in the power of horoscopes, but they are fun to follow.

A person's horoscope, or birth chart, as it is also called, depends on the time of the calendar year in which they were born. The year is divided into twelve sections, which make up the **zodiac.** The zodiac is the circular chart on which horoscopes are based. Each section is called a **sign.** The zodiac is connected to twelve constellations in the night skies.

Horoscopes and astrology began with the Greeks thousands of years ago. They were used to predict when to plant and when to harvest their crops. The word *astrology* is a Greek word that means "science of the stars." It is said that Greek people first noticed how the position of the sun influenced the seasons as well as the growing cycles. This observation then developed into the belief that the position of the sun and the planets also had an effect on a person's life and on what future events would happen to them. Some astrologers believed that a

horoscope would not predict the future, but would predict possible influences the planets had on a person's life.

People held these beliefs until modern-day religions developed. Once religions developed, most people did not take the idea of astrology as seriously. For many centuries, horoscopes and astrology were studied only by small groups of people. Interest started to increase in horoscopes when newspapers began to feature them. Today, almost all newspapers feature daily horoscopes. Most people think of astrology as a form of entertainment, rather than believing in it the way people used to centuries ago. The most commonly held belief today is that astrology is more superstition than an accurate way to predict the future.

Here are the signs of the zodiac.

If you were born between March 21 and April 19, then your sign is Aries. Arians are said to be confident and intelligent. They are also said to be impatient and selfish at times.

If you were born between April 20 and May 20, then your sign is Taurus. Taureans are said to be dependable and loyal. They are also said to be stubborn and self-indulgent at times.

If you were born between May 21 and June 20, then your sign is Gemini. Geminis are said to be harmonious and agreeable. They are also said to be fickle and gossipy at times.

If you were born between June 21 and July 22, then your sign is Cancer. Cancers are said to be sensitive and protective. They are also said to be moody and shrewd at times.

If you were born between July 23 and August 22, then your sign is Leo. Leos are said to be honest and brave. They are also said to be braggers at times.

If you were born between August 23 and September 22, then your sign is Virgo. Virgos are said to be modest and hard-working. They are also said to be irritable and sloppy at times.

If you were between September 23 and October 22, then your sign is Libra. Librans are said to be charming and romantic. They are also said to be flirty and overbearing at times.

If you were born between October 23 and November 22, then your sign is Scorpio. Scorpions are said to be good concentrators. They are also said to be secretive and unnerving at times.

If you were born between November 23 and December 21, then your sign is Sagittarius. Sagittarians are said to be optimistic and adaptable. They are also said to be short-tempered and indulgent at times.

If you were born between December 22 and January 19, then your sign is Capricorn. Capricorns are said to be realistic and cautious. They are also said to be egotistical and critical at times.

If you were born between January 20 and February 19, then your sign is Aquarius. Aquarians are said to be cooperative and thoughtful. They are also said to be rude and insecure at times.

If you were born between February 20 and March 20, then your sign is Pisces. Pisceans are said to be caring and helpful. They are also said to be dependent and blameful of others at times.

NON-FICTION STYLE: *SUMMARIZING*

Summarizing is an important skill to have when you are doing research. Summarizing means explaining information in your own words.

When you summarize, you find the main idea(s) of something you have read and then put it into your own words. When you summarize, you are trying to include only the main point(s), not supporting details. Summaries are usually shorter than the original paragraph you have read. Here are some tips to help you summarize.

- Do not write down everything from the article.
- Make sure you write enough for people to understand your meaning and subject.
- Do not give complete sentences. Write in point form.
- Find the main ideas, read them, and then explain the main idea to yourself, using your own words.
- Focus on key details, the ones needed to give an understanding.
- Use key words and phrases.

Extended Learning Sheet: Summarizing

A hint to help in summarizing is to look at any headings or subheadings in an article. Often, these headings contain main ideas. Charts and diagrams will also have headings. Look at the main paragraphs and charts in your article, and then reread them. Create a heading for each one, then list some important key details to support that heading (write these details in short point form).

Paragraph #_____

Heading:

_____

Key Details

_____

_____

_____

Paragraph #_____

Heading:

_____

Key Details

_____

_____

_____

Chart #_____

Heading:

_____

Chart #_____

Heading:

_____

TOTEM POLES: GIANT STORYTELLERS

We often think of totem poles as interesting decorations, but totem poles are much more than that. Totem poles have meaning. They tell a story or an event in the First Nations culture.

Not all totem poles are the same. The way a totem pole is designed is often based on its purpose. The biggest mistake people make when viewing totem poles is assuming they were carved for religious purposes. This is not true. Traditional totem poles were never carved for religious ceremonies or worshipped as religious objects.

Here are some of the most common reasons for carving a totem pole.

Memorial Poles	Mortuary Poles
Erected to honour an important person at the time of death. A crest would represent the person's clan (family).	Similar to memorial poles except an open section is carved in the back to hold the remains of the deceased.
Potlatch Poles	**Heraldic Poles**
Raised during a potlatch ceremony. A Potlatch is an important occasion that marks significant events in the tribe.	Proclaim the social standing of a wealthy person or the head of the house. Attached to the front of a building with an opening for an entrance.
House Poles	**Ridicule or Shame Poles**
Part of a pillar inside the house, often carved with crests of the owner.	Erected to shame a person or family for failure to pay a debt or for breaking a trust.

The figures on a totem pole are put on there for a reason. Usually, the carvings are of animals. Each animal represents a different idea. Here are some of the most common ones.

Killer Whale Most powerful sea mammal, a symbol of fantasy and superstition.	**Raven** The most important of creatures, known as the trickster.
Frog A watchman who brings good fortune: one of the most powerful spirits.	**Bear** A symbol of power and wisdom.
Eagle The symbol of power, friendship, peace, and honour.	**Hummingbird** A symbol of good fortune and good weather to come.
Wolf Known as reserved because it was a good hunter, is associated with the special spirit a person needed to be a successful hunter.	**Hawk** A spirit of the supernatural, used to represent Thunderbird, the most powerful of all spirits—like a chief.

Other birds, such as cormorants, cranes, owls, and loons, appeared on totem poles. Groundhogs and otters also appeared on them. Sea animals, such as shark, seal, and sea lion, were found on totem poles. Butterflies, dragonflies, mosquitoes, and even sea monsters were on totem poles.

Traditionally, totem poles were carved by artists who were trained in the art. A clan chief would select the figures he wanted on the pole and have the artist create it. Originally, totem poles were carved with tools made from stone, bone, or shell. Before paints were available, the artist used very little colour. Those colours that were used were created by the artist from a variety of sources. Crushed salmon eggs were used in the mixing of the paints before the artist applied it to the totem pole.

- soot, graphite, or charcoal were used for black
- red ochre produced reds, browns, and yellow
- copper sulphide produced blue-green
- baked clam shells and burned limestone provided white

The totem poles were carved and painted horizontally, but then came the difficult task of raising the totem pole. It took great skill and cooperation to raise a totem pole, and usually involved traditions and ceremonies. Often, it required more than a hundred men to carry the pole to the site it would occupy. The base of the pole was placed over a deep hole with a trench extending out from it. The top of the pole was then raised, using wooden supports and ropes. The ropes were attached to the upper part of the pole and passed over the supporting frame. Everybody would pull on the ropes at once to raise the pole to its upright position. Once a totem pole was raised, it remained there even if the people moved to a new village location.

THE GRAND CANYON
One of the Wonders of the World

The Grand Canyon is immense. The deep cavern is 446 kilometres (277 miles) long, up to 29 kilometres (18 miles) wide, and more than 1500 metres (5000 feet) deep. The canyon covers over 1,200,000 acres. The six-million-year-old Grand Canyon is made up of buttes, plateaus, and mesas that cover two-billion-year-old rock. It is located in northwestern Arizona. A part of it on each side is known as Grand Canyon National Park, which has four million tourists visiting each year. It is often called one of the seven wonders of the world.

The Grand Canyon was created by the Colorado River. The water rushing through the rocky area created erosion. The river started the erosion about six million years ago, but the rock that makes up the canyon is two billion years old. The river continues to flow through the bottom sections of the canyon.

Parts of the northern rim of the canyon are forested because the elevation there is higher and the region gets more moisture in the form of snow each year. Vegetation in the deep parts of the valley is mainly desert plants, such as agaves and Spanish bayonet. There is very little soil for plants to grow in the area. Desert plants like the cacti have adapted to living in the hot, dry environment of the Grand Canyon. Cacti have wide and shallow roots that allow the plants to soak up moisture after a rain.

The climate of the plateau region, the flat area above the canyon, is severe. It experiences seasons with extreme heat and cold. The northern rim of the canyon has snow for half the year, making it very difficult for tourists to visit this region easily. The canyon floor becomes very hot in summer, and rarely experiences frost in the wintertime.

The canyon is home to many different wildlife. Bighorn sheep like the rocky slopes of the inner canyon, which keep them safe from predators. The Bighorn feed on grasses and other flora in the area. The Grand Canyon is also a safe place for endangered species such as the California Condor bird. Reptiles are common in the desert-like conditions of the canyon. Reptiles such as the Gila monster and the chuckwalla live in the area. The Gila monster is the largest and only venomous lizard in the United States. The venom of the Gila monster can be painful but rarely causes death. A chuckwalla is a large lizard with loose folds of skin around its upper body. The canyon is also home to many different snake species.

Butte

A hill that rises abruptly from the surrounding area and has sloping sides and a flat top.

Plateau

An elevated, comparatively level expanse of land.

Mesa

A broad, flat-topped elevation with one or more cliff-like sides, common in the southwest United States.

ALL ABOUT HORSES

Horses are not all the same. There many different types (or breeds) of horses. There are three main groups of horses and about 100 breeds. A **pony** stands 10 to 14 hands (approximately 100 to 150 centimetres) and weighs 300 to 850 pounds (135 to 380 kilograms). A **light horse** stands 14 to 17 hands (150 to 175 centimetres) and weighs 800 to 1300 pounds (360 to 590 kilograms). A **draft horse** stands 15 to 19 hands (160 to 190 centimetres) and weighs 1500 to 2600 pounds (700 to 1200 kilograms). Ponies are considered small horses. The best-known breed is the Shetland pony. The Arabian is one of the oldest breeds of light horses. One of the most common breeds of draft horses is the Clydesdale.

Horses have been very important to people. They have been used by people for centuries. Since ponies were smaller types of horses, they were used to work in mines to get into places where larger horses could not fit. Light horses were one of the first forms of transportation for people. Light horses were also used for pulling light vehicles and ranch work. For many centuries, the horse was used to ride in battles and wars. Draft horses were used for pulling heavy loads and for farm work. They are not as common as they once were, having been replaced by modern-day machinery. Today, horses are used primarily for sports such as racing, show competition, rodeos, and simple riding for pleasure.

Everyone is familiar with the look of the horse but there is more to its appearance than you may realize. One of the features of a horse that is most noticeable is its tail. A horse's tail is very important to him. Not only does it act as a fly swatter in summer, it keeps his "bottom" warm in winter! The area between a horse's hind legs is the only part not kept warm by hair, so it loses the greatest amount of warmth if left exposed by too much trimming. There are 52 different parts to the horse's body. Some of these parts include the hock, muzzle, and flank. Many horses have white markings on their faces. All the markings on horses have special names. The markings themselves may vary in shape, but are similar on most horses. The names for the markings are used by horse people to identify different horses, which may otherwise appear the same in colour. While some horses may be the same colour, horses can be many colours. In fact, many times horses are more commonly identified by their colour rather than by their breed.

The horse begins life as a foal (male) or filly (female). During the first year, the foal/filly has very long legs, compared to the rest of its body. After two months, the foal/filly sheds its milk hairs. Two months later, it will stop drinking milk from its mother. After it no longer drinks milk from its mother, it is called a horse. The foal/filly is born with no teeth. As it gets older, the horse grows teeth. By the time the foal/filly is six to nine months, the young horse has all its milk teeth. At five to six years of age, the horse replaces its milk teeth with its permanent teeth. You can tell how old a horse is by its teeth. At 12 months the horse is known as a yearling. At 12 months the baby horse is still uncoordinated, but its body is beginning to grow to match its legs. A horse goes into its middle years at the age of 5 to 10 years. By then, the horse is fully formed. After this stage, it goes on to its late years. A horse's lifespan is often well into its 20s.

Horses, like any other animal, have certain behaviours that make them unique. The horse is naturally a grass eater. Horses may spend around 11 to 13 hours a day, grazing on grass. Horses generally sleep standing up, but spend some time lying down if they feel safe enough. Some people do not realize that horses can swim. Many really enjoy the water! Horses have very good "homing" senses and can find their way back from a very long way away. Horses that live in groups will often make friends with other horses and will often have a special "buddy."

Appaloosa – a breed of horse with spots, any colour mixed with white.

Bay – dark red to deep brown with black points.

Black – two types of black: fading black and jet black.

Brown – black with brown muzzle.

Buckskin – coat colour to a yellow, cream, or gold while keeping the black mane, tail, ears, legs.

Chestnut – a reddish/yellowish brown with no black points.

Dun – yellowish brown with a dorsal stripe along the back and occasionally zebra stripings on the legs.

Pinto – multicoloured with large patches of brown, white, and/or black and white.

Blaze	**Bald Face**	**Star**	**Snip**	**Race**	**Strip**
broad marking down the front of the horse's face	marking that covers most of the horse's face	found high up between the eyes, often a diamond shape	small mark on the muzzle	long, wavy or irregular stripe	long, straight marking down the horse's nose

NON-FICTION STYLE: *INFERRING AND DRAWING CONCLUSIONS*

Writers often tell you more than just what is in the words printed on the page. They give you hints or clues that help you "read between the lines." Using these clues helps you have a deeper understanding of your reading. As a reader, you must go beyond the actual words and details to see other meanings the details suggest.

Each day you make inferences. Making an inference means making a judgment. If you infer that something has happened, you do not see, hear, feel, smell, or taste the event. But, from what you know, it makes sense to think that it has happened. Making inferences means choosing the most likely explanation from the facts at hand.

In drawing conclusions, you are really focusing on the main meaning of things —what is important, why it is important, how one event influences another, how one happening leads to another. Simply getting the facts in reading is not enough—you must think about what those facts mean to you.

Extended Learning Sheet: Inferring and Drawing Conclusions

The following chart will help you make inferences and draw conclusions. Use it after you have read an article.

Article: _____

I believe the message the author is trying to get across to me is …

_____

_____

_____

_____

I can explain this because …

_____

_____

_____

_____

The Curse of King Tut

King Tutankamen (King Tut) lived about 3300 years ago. He reigned very briefly in Egypt until he died at only 18 years of age. During early wars in Egypt, monuments to King Tut were destroyed, and the location of his tomb was forgotten.

In the 20th century, when archaeologists started digging for the tomb of another king, they accidentally came across part of King Tut's tomb. Many tombs had been raided for their treasures but Tut's was perfectly hidden from robbers, so his considerable treasure was untouched.

In November 1922, the archaeologist Howard Carter was ready to open King Tut's tomb in Luxor's Valley of the Kings. Eventually, his workers dug down four metres below their existing dig and found an entrance in the rock that led to a passageway. They cleaned out the rubble, and found a sealed stone doorway.

This was exciting news, so Howard Carter immediately invited his financier, Lord Carnarvon, to come to the site for the opening of the tomb. Carter and Carnarvon were present when all the rubble was removed to reveal the stone door of King Tutankhamen. The door was opened. There was magnificent treasure in the rooms of Tut's tomb—Lord Carnarvon himself opened this inner door. King Tut's mummified remains were inside three coffins. The outer two coffins were made of hammered gold fitted to wooden frames, and the innermost coffin was made of solid gold.

Another Story—The Curse!

But another story soon started to unfold. Because mummies have been associated with many magical powers throughout history, some of the mummies found in Egypt were ground into a fine powder and sold as a mystical mummy powder. It was believed the powder had magical healing powers. But when King Tut's tomb was opened in 1922, the journalists reported that an inscription near the door of the tomb read, "Death shall come on swift wings to him that touches the tomb of the Pharaoh." The curse of the mummy began when many terrible events occurred after the discovery of King Tut's tomb.

Lord Carnarvon, the person who funded the discovery of King Tut's tomb, died shortly after the discovery. In the spring of 1923, he was bitten on the cheek by a mosquito. It soon became infected when he was shaving and Lord Carnarvon became ill. He suffered a high fever and chills. A doctor was sent to examine him but he arrived too late and Lord Carnarvon died. At that exact moment, the lights in Cairo mysteriously went out.

Once Carnarvon died, the stories began growing. People said King Tut wanted vengeance and put a mummy's curse on those who had entered the tomb. Other stories were soon reported, one being that a cobra killed Howard Carter's pet canary after the discovery of King Tut's tomb. What is interesting is that Howard Carter, the explorer who actually discovered the tomb, lived long after this major discovery. He spent his remaining years logging and recording every artefact found in the tomb. Why didn't he suffer the curse of the mummy? He was, after all, the first to enter the tomb. Did King Tut's tomb really unleash a curse?

Modern-Day Research

Since that time, scientists have continued to study King Tut's tomb. In 1986, a French doctor, Caroline Stenger-Phillip, explained that the tomb most likely contained a mould from the fruits and vegetables in the tomb. The mould formed bacteria on the walls and dust particles that could be highly allergenic. Breathing in these particles could have serious effects on the human body. More recent research also points out that Carnarvon was not in the best of health.

Six years after the discovery, twelve of the expedition members were dead. Howard Carter died at the reasonable age (for those days) of 66. Dr. Douglas Derry, who dissected the mummy, died when he was over the age of 80. Alfred Lucas, the chemist who analyzed tissues from the mummy, died at 79.

Other details in the stories have been looked at in recent years. For example, the cobra snake is a common snake in Egypt and many high winds cause numerous blackouts in Cairo.

Fact or fiction, the curse of the mummy seems to interest people even today. Do you believe in the curse of the mummy?

THE BERMUDA TRIANGLE: FACT OR LEGEND?

One of the legends of the sea that is told to this very day is the story of the Bermuda Triangle, where ships and airplanes seem to disappear more often than in other parts of the ocean. The Bermuda Triangle, also known as the Devil's Triangle, is a triangular area in the Atlantic Ocean bordering Miami, Bermuda, and Puerto Rico. Legend has it that many people, ships, and planes have mysteriously vanished in this area, never to be seen again. Of course, this area is known for hurricanes and high waves.

Does the Bermuda Triangle deserve the title of "graveyard of the Atlantic"?

Many ideas have been proposed to explain the so-called mysteries of these missing ships and planes. Aliens, leftover power sources from the fabled sunken city of Atlantis, evil humans with anti-gravity machines or other strange devices, and holes from a fourth dimension are ideas often mentioned by people such as fantasy and science-fiction writers. Other possible reasons have included magnetic fields, pirates, and strange weather storms.

How many planes and ships have actually disappeared in the Bermuda Triangle? The answer depends how you define the Bermuda Triangle. Some people think of it as a much larger area stretching out over the ocean. With this definition, more sea accidents can be included. Another consideration is how

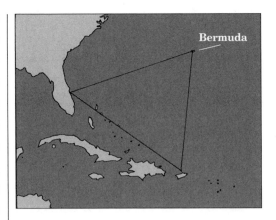

long people think the Bermuda Triangle has been in existence. Some people say strange occurrences have been taking place for the past 500 years. Again, if you include all this time, there would be more wrecks than if you believe the incidents in the Bermuda Triangle have occurred only in recent times. The United States Coast Guard is closest to the triangle and responds to any at-sea emergencies. According to their records, more than 50 ships and 20 planes in the past hundred years have been lost. However, they point out that they have responded to over 8000 calls of SOS in the area and safely helped them.

People with little experience at sea may think the number of wrecks in this area is extraordinary but those people knowledgeable about the ocean say that, given its size, location, and the amount of traffic in this area, this is not a number out of the ordinary. Investigations have not produced scientific evidence of any unusual weather patterns in the area, but it is a part of the ocean, along with many other areas, that does experience severe tropical storms.

Perhaps the more interesting story is how the mystery of the Bermuda Triangle started. Many people give credit to writers. Over the years, numerous articles, books, and television programs have promoted the mystery of the Bermuda Triangle. In fact, the name "Bermuda Triangle" was invented by a writer named Vincent Gaddis, who wrote an article called "The Deadly Bermuda Triangle," which appeared in the February 1964 issue of *Argosy*, a magazine for fiction. In the book, *The Bermuda Triangle Mystery —Solved*, author Larry Kusche tells us he spent an enormous amount of time actually going through legitimate records of alleged disappearances and wrecks. He found that many of the strange accidents could be explained. Many writers did not check facts but based their writing on stories and legends. Often, a writer would state a ship or plane had disappeared in "calm seas" when the record showed a raging storm that day. Others said ships had "mysteriously vanished" when their remains had actually been found and the cause of their sinking explained.

The real-life story that seems to have started the modern-day legend of

the Bermuda Triangle is the disappearance of five Navy planes, known as Flight 19. The small planes vanished on a training mission in a harsh storm in 1945. Researchers believe they vanished because the lead plane's compass failed and the other planes were not properly equipped with navigation devices. The group became lost over the ocean in the raging storm and ran out of fuel. No mysterious forces were reported, yet a legend grew around these missing pilots.

In 1945, planes did not have the equipment pilots have today for knowing their location. A pilot had to know his bearings and make calculations for locations based on distance and speed. With no landmarks over the ocean, it was easy to get lost.

Is the mystery of the Bermuda Triangle based on fact or on legend? That is for you to determine in your own mind.

THE IMPORTANCE OF RECYCLING

Why do I have to recycle? What difference does it make if I do or don't? Can one person make that much of a difference? Learn more about recycling and you may be able to answer some of these questions.

Recycling prevents greenhouse gases from polluting the air. Greenhouse gases are pollution that enters the air from factories that make materials. The polluted air affects plant life, which has an effect on us, since plants give off oxygen for us to breathe.

Recycling just one aluminum can saves enough electricity to light a 100-watt bulb for three and a half hours. Recycling a tonne of glass equals the saving of nine litres of fuel oil. Recycling one glass container saves enough energy to light a 100-watt bulb for four hours. Recycling used aluminum cans requires only about 5 percent of the energy needed to produce a new aluminum can. Every kilogram of steel recycled saves enough energy to light a 60-watt bulb for over 26 hours. When we use less energy, we do not have to go searching the earth for new sources of energy.

Recycling of each tonne of paper saves 17 trees and 7000 litres of water. This means there are more trees around for us and the animals and also more water for us to drink. If all morning newspapers in North America were recycled for one day, the equivalent of 41,000 trees would be saved and 6 million tonnes of waste would never end up in landfills. Landfills take up valuable space and they are only used for storing garbage.

Recycling reduces the need for landfills. Landfills can last longer and that means natural habitats are not destroyed.

Recycling does save our environment. If we recycle used motor oil, we keep it out of rivers, lakes, streams, and even groundwater. In many cases, that means keeping it out of our drinking water, off our beaches, and away from wildlife. Recycling the motor oil from one oil change protects a million litres of drinking water—or, a year's supply for 50 people. Imagine! One oil change can affect that many people!

Recycling is "good business." Recycling often produces better products than those made of new materials. For example, the tin in "tin" cans is more valuable after being recycled. Making new products out of recycled steel uses 74 percent less energy than making new tin cans from new steel. By turning waste into renewed products, we also create jobs for people.

We can even recycle many items we may not normally think of reusing. For example, we rarely think of clothes as garbage, but approximately 500 million kilograms of clothing material sit in North American landfills. Instead of throwing those clothes out, we can donate them to charity or use the material for new projects.

Five Easy Steps to Recycle a Glass Container

1. Remove the cap, lid, or ring (you need not worry about removing the paper label).
2. Rinse out the container.
3. Dry the container or let it drain.
4. Place the container in a sturdy cardboard box.
5. When the box is full, take it to a recycling centre.

GLOSSARY OF TERMS

Activating Activity	A form of a mini-lesson that generates discussion and thought processes such as the discovery of new ideas.
Categorize	The ability to place into a group, or classify, according to a specific characteristic, idea, or rule.
Cause and Effect	A system of comprehension and reasoning. The reader determines reasons for a particular event and the consequences of such an action.
Classify	The process of arranging words and ideas into groups (categories established according to defined criteria).
Compare	The process of examining two ideas and explaining a system for their similarity.
Contrast	The process of examining two related ideas and explaining how they differ.
Discussion	A genre of non-fiction. The piece of writing looks at both sides of an idea and draws a conclusion, using the facts as a basis for the choice.
Element	One of the four main components of non-fiction. Physical features used to assist in conveying a message. Bold type, diagrams, and sidebars are some of the elements used in non-fiction.
Explanatory	A genre of non-fiction. The writing tells what happened or how something works, and provides reasons.
Fact	A statement that can be proven and tested or checked for accuracy.

Genre	A type of non-fiction based on purpose or intent of the information the author is sharing.
Graphic Organizer	A diagram or picture to show information, used to gain meaning in reading, writing, and speaking. Timelines and charts are graphic organizers.
Inference	The process of coming to come to a conclusion (about an idea), based on existing evidence or what is already known. It is a part of reasoning skills.
Info Fiction	Also known as blended text. A genre of non-fiction in which the author implies conclusions based on factual content. Biographies are often a form of blended text.
Instructional	A genre of non-fiction that uses steps to describe how something is made or how it works.
Non-Fiction	A form of writing relying heavily on factual content.
Opinion	A statement of belief or a judgment that cannot be proven true or false.
Paraphrase	The use of your own words to explain another person's ideas. It is also a reading strategy to help make sense of ideas.
Relating	A genre of non-fiction. The author retells information or events for the audience (readers).
Report	A genre of non-fiction. The author describes something or some event. Written in present tense.
Rubric	A scoring guide for assessment. The rating scale offers specific criteria created by the assessor to measure achievement and performance.
Structure	A format used in non-fiction writing. The format may have a specific purpose and take on specific elements that help identify it. Editorials, travelogues, letters, and brochures are a few existing structures in non-fiction.
Style	A way of writing that helps the author create the tone and intent of the writing.
Summary	The process of stating an existing idea by using different words from the original text. Summaries use less words than the original but the content remains the same even if the language is different.

BIBLIOGRAPHY

During the development of our guided reading program, we read much professional literature to help us formulate our thoughts on the subject. Below, you will find further professional reading that can help you continue on your own personal journey on the subject of guided reading.

Atwell, Nancy. *In the Middle: Writing, Reading, and Learning with Adolescents.* Portsmouth, NH: Heinemann, 1987.

Burns, Bonnie. *Guided Reading.* Thousand Oaks, CA: Corwin Press, 2001.

Fountas, Irene C., and Gay Su Pinnell. *Guiding Readers and Writers (Grades 3–6): Teaching Comprehension, Genre, and Content Literacy.* Portsmouth, NH: Heinemann, 2001.

Harvey, Stephanie. *Nonfiction Matters.* York, ME: Stenhouse Publishers, 1998.

Holdaway, Don. *The Foundations of Literacy.* New York, NY: Scholastic, 1984.

Jamison, Lori. *Guided Reading Basics.* Markham, ON: Pembroke Publishers, 2003.

Schwartz, Susan, and Maxine Bone. *Retelling, Relating, Reflecting Beyond the Three Rs.* New York, NY: Irwin Publishers, 1995.

Saunders-Smith, Gail. *The Ultimate Guided Reading How-To Book: Building Literacy through Small-Group Instruction.* Chicago, IL: Zephyr Press, 2002.

Visser, Evangelyn, Gary M. Hanggi, and Sara Davis Powell. *Guided Reading in a Balanced Program: A Professional's Guide.* Westminster, CA: Teacher Created Resources, 1999.

The Wright Group, ed. *Guided Reading, A Practical Approach for Teachers.* DeSoto, TX: Wright Group Publishing, 1995.

INDEX